Cambridge Elements ≡

Elements in Earth System Governance
edited by
Frank Biermann
Utrecht University
Aarti Gupta
Wageningen University

FOREST GOVERNANCE: HYDRA OR CHLORIS?

Bas Arts
Wageningen University & Research
Radboud University Nijmegen

CAMBRIDGE
UNIVERSITY PRESS

CAMBRIDGE
UNIVERSITY PRESS

University Printing House, Cambridge CB2 8BS, United Kingdom

One Liberty Plaza, 20th Floor, New York, NY 10006, USA

477 Williamstown Road, Port Melbourne, VIC 3207, Australia

314–321, 3rd Floor, Plot 3, Splendor Forum, Jasola District Centre, New Delhi – 110025, India

103 Penang Road, #05–06/07, Visioncrest Commercial, Singapore 238467

Cambridge University Press is part of the University of Cambridge.

It furthers the University's mission by disseminating knowledge in the pursuit of education, learning, and research at the highest international levels of excellence.

www.cambridge.org
Information on this title: www.cambridge.org/9781108810975
DOI: 10.1017/9781108863551

First published 2021

A catalogue record for this publication is available from the British Library.

ISBN 978-1-108-81097-5 Paperback
ISSN 2631-7818 (online)
ISSN 2631-780X (print)

Forest Governance: Hydra or Chloris?

Elements in Earth System Governance

DOI: 10.1017/9781108863551
First published online: October 2021

Bas Arts
Wageningen University & Research
Radboud University Nijmegen
Author for correspondence: Bas Arts, bas.arts@wur.nl

Abstract: Many forest-related problems are considered relevant today. One might think of deforestation, illegal logging and biodiversity loss. Yet, many governance initiatives have been initiated to work on their solutions. This Element takes stock of these issues and initiatives by analysing different forest governance modes, shifts and norms, and by studying five cases (forest sector governance, forest legality, forest certification, forest conservation, participatory forest management). Special focus is on performance: are the many forest governance initiatives able to change established practices of forest decline (Chloris worldview) or are they doomed to fail (Hydra worldview)? The answer will be *both*, depending on geographies and local conditions. The analyses are guided by discursive institutionalism and philosophical pragmatism. This title is also available as Open Access on Cambridge Core.

This Element also has a video abstract: www.cambridge.org/forestgovernance

Keywords: forest governance, governance modes, shifts and norms, governance discourses, institutional arrangements, performance

ISBNs: 9781108810975 (PB), 9781108863551 (OC)
ISSNs: 2631-7818 (online), 2631-780X (print)

Contents

1 Introduction: Hydra and Chloris Worldviews

*When someone says that he or she adopts
a governance perspective, this is the
beginning, rather than the end, of the
discussion.* (Pierre and Peters, 2000, p. 37)

Ideally, this Element gives you answers to all your questions about forest governance. But, as the quote above indicates, governance is an elusive and contested concept, so any conclusion arrived at will subsequently result in new discussions. Moreover, guided by philosophical pragmatism, this Element tries to find a synthesis of mainstream and critical perspectives on forest governance, a quest that some of my colleagues will definitely challenge. While trying to arrive at this middle ground, the Element sketches various discourses, institutions and practices of forest governance at national and international levels. The following cases will be dealt with: Forest Sector Governance (FSG), Forest Law Enforcement, Governance and Trade (FLEGT), Reducing Emissions from Deforestation and Forest Degradation (REDD+), Forest Certification (FC) and Participatory Forest Management (PFM). As such, besides its theoretical ambitions, the Element also offers an empirical overview of the field, albeit with an inevitable European bias, given my personal background, research experience and academic perspective.

First though, what is so special about *forest* governance? Do we need a small handbook in addition to those on resource governance, environmental governance and governance in general? Well, forests differ from many other natural resources (like those of the open seas) and many other environmental issues (like those of the atmosphere) in that they belong to national territories of nation states. Although many would consider forests and their problems (such as deforestation and degradation) global issues and concerns, others strongly disagree, and oppose any global governance response by the international community (for an overview of this debate see Fernández-Blanco et al., 2019; Giessen, 2013; Humphreys, 1996; Kolk, 1996; Sotirov et al., 2020). Yet, many global governance initiatives have been launched – from declarations, programmes, strategies and labelling schemes to codes of conduct – albeit mostly voluntary and non-legally binding in nature. Dimitrov and colleagues (2007) therefore speak of a 'non-regime' on forests; that there is a need for a strong global regime to effectively address forest-related problems, but according to these authors, what we observe are voluntary, mainly symbolic rules. This makes the topic of forest governance extremely interesting to study: on the one hand, a 'non-regime', while on the other many things are happening on the ground (as this Element will show). The topic is also a laboratory of governance experimentation, given initiatives like PFM, FLEGT and REDD+.

The subtitle of the Element requires some explanation. Hydra and Chloris are figures from Greek mythology and are used in this Element as two overarching worldviews on forest governance in the scholarly literature; one overall *critical* about governance theory and *pessimistic* about the potential of governance performance, and one overall *supportive* and *optimistic*. Hydra is the multi-headed, serpent-like beast that 'half god – half human' Heracles (a son of Zeus) has to fight to complete his twelve labours (see Figure 1). Every time Heracles chops off one of the heads, it immediately regrows double, and continues attacking him. Eventually, Heracles is able to defeat the monster with the help of his cousin Lalaos, who uses fire (instead of a sword) to avoid the regrowth of heads (which is, by the way, a classic example of 'thinking outside the box'). Chloris, from the ancient Greek word *khloris* or 'green', is the goddess of flowers (see Figure 2). Originally, she is a nymph but after being abducted by Zephyrus, the god of the Western Wind, she marries him. Because she is so beautiful, colourful and fond of flowers and nature, Zephyrus builds her a beautiful garden and turns her into the immortal goddess of flowers. Later, the Romans renamed her Flora (which sounds much more familiar to us).

Hydra is sometimes used as a metaphor in conflict studies and crisis management literature (Held et al., 2010). It refers to situations where the solution of one conflict or crisis is the foundation for a new one, or multiple ones – just like

Figure 1 Heracles fights the Hydra (source: iStock, reprint permitted)

Figure 2 Chloris, the goddess of flowers (source: iStock, reprint permitted)

the reappearing head being chopped off. In the forest governance literature, only one reference to the multi-headed beast was identified: 'The emergence of the REDD+ Hydra' (Martone, 2010). Since REDD+ is dealt with in Section 5 of this Element, it suffices to state here that it covers reducing greenhouse gas emissions from deforestation and forest degradation in order to contribute to the mitigation of human-induced climate change. In this instance, Martone refers to the situation around 2010 where seven initiatives on REDD+ quickly emerged in parallel at Conferences of the Parties of the United Nations Framework Convention on Climate Change (UNFCCC), each expressing different prefer-ences for a REDD+ mechanism and thus speaking with different voices –

a modern Hydra. However, since REDD+ became part of the Paris Agreement in 2015 these divergent views have largely converged.

This usage of the metaphor is close to the one in this Element. The point is as follows: the field of forest governance shows increasing numbers of initiatives at all levels (local, national, global) to reform, innovate or transform classical forest policy, programmes and projects in order to enhance the sustainable use and conservation of forests (Fernández-Blanco et al., 2019; McDermott et al., 2010; Pülzl et al., 2013). In metaphorical terms: old heads need to be chopped off, but they quickly reappear. So, reforms and innovations have a hard time to truly change established practices, let alone reaching a point that real transformation can actually take off (Humphreys, 2006). Alternatively, it can be concluded that many reforms and innovations are not really *meant* to change established practices. These are just 'paper initiatives' of governors who want to maintain the status quo, but design symbolic policies to please and co-opt a certain constituency (Dimitrov, 2005). Part of the metaphor too is the violent scenery and associated negative connotation Hydra expresses. In a similar vein, several scholars sketch an unfavourable image of the many forest governance initiatives that emerge; these lead to messiness in, and fragmentation of, the domain (Giessen, 2013; Soto Golcher, 2020). And according to some scholars, the many initiatives even imply a *decrease* of governance capacity, since they are an expression of neo-liberalism, of outsourcing public duties to private entities, and hence reduced government control and greater business and market powers (Fletcher, 2010). No surprise that these scholars deem such a development a negative one – 'It smells' (like the poisoning breath of the Hydra).

As far as I know, Chloris is not used as a metaphor in governance or management studies, let alone in the forest governance literature. The only hit I found concerning 'Chloris' AND 'forest governance' was a reference to the bird *Chloris Chloris* – the European greenfinch – that lives at forest edges or in parks with trees. In this Element, the metaphor is used to sketch the opposite picture of forest governance compared to that of the Hydra. The many forest governance initiatives now take the shape of a beautiful bouquet of flowers that smells wonderful. 'Let a thousand flowers bloom' is the message, some of which will perform better than others, of course, but at least results are to be expected from the bouquet as a whole (Arts and Babili, 2013; Rayner et al., 2010). In addition, new flowers will grow and be added to the bouquet, that is, new pathways will be explored, which might show more or less performance of initiatives through processes of trial and error and learning (Overdedest and Zeitling, 2014). Overall, the picture carries a much more positive connotation: the world becomes a better place due to these forest governance initiatives.

To further deepen our understanding of the Chloris and Hydra worldviews, they can be considered *multi-layered* (see Table 1). First of all, there are *core beliefs* (Sabatier, 2007) about the potential for progress through governance reform and technical solutions. For example, Charles Mann (2018) distinguishes the *wizard* from the *prophet* in his book on two duelling visions of the world's future, whereby the wizard is the optimistic believer in progress, while the prophet expects doom for our overpopulated and overexploited planet. To view the world as a wizard or as a prophet is a core belief in the sense that it generally circumvents consciousness, rationality and deliberation; it is just there, deeply rooted in our state of mind (although people can change their beliefs, but over the course of a lifetime, not simply overnight).

The *second layer* comes close to what Cox (1981) calls *problem-solving theories* versus *critical theories*. The first group takes the social order and its institutions for granted and tries to find solutions for given problems within that order, such as poverty, inequality and environmental issues. There is a strong belief that this social order can be reformed in such a way that these problems are addressed effectively, and often in mutual coherence (*win-wins*), so that the public good, at least for most people, is finally attained. The second ensemble of critical theories is sceptical of such reformism, because the structural root cause of these problems is not addressed, that of the capitalist political economy. This order thrives on economic growth and expansion, which while benefiting so many people, also comes with many problems, such as inequality, poverty and overexploitation (*trade-offs*). Mitigating these will not work by addressing sectoral issues within the given social order, as the critical theorists argue, but only by fundamentally transforming the system as a whole.

Table 1 Chloris and Hydra as multi-layered worldviews

Multi-layered worldviews	Chloris	Hydra
Beliefs	Wizard ('progress scenario')	Prophet ('doom scenario')
Theories	Problem-solving (sectoral solutions; win-win situations)	Critical (trade-offs; system change is needed)
Facts	Confirmation bias (e.g. less deforestation over time; more forest protection; SFM progresses)	Confirmation bias (e.g. biodiversity loss aggravates; marginalisation of forest-dependent people)

The *third layer* is about how one relates to the *factual world*. Indeed, different facts may be mobilised to confirm one's own worldview, or to undermine the other, but on top of that, similar facts may be interpreted distinctly. For example, the Food and Agriculture Organization's (FAO) (2020) latest Global Forest Assessment (GFA) reports that the rate of global deforestation has reduced over the last decades – from a net annual loss of 7.8 million hectares (ha) of forests in the 1990s to minus 5.2 million ha in the 2000s and to minus 4.7 million ha in the 2010s – while the number of countries that have adopted forest laws, Sustainable Forest Management (SFM) principles and National Forest Programmes (NFP) has increased over time. A Chloris interpretation would probably welcome these figures and conclude that forest governance initiatives do obviously make a difference. A Hydra interpretation would probably critique FAO's 'aggregated net deforestation data', because these – by including loss and expansion of *all* forests worldwide, primary, secondary and plantations – hide the ongoing *increase* of tropical deforestation in many regions and the ongoing *loss* of primary forests and of forest biodiversity. Also, net or gross forest area data *themselves* could be critiqued, because these do not address the root causes and drivers of deforestation, like poverty, agricultural expansion, road infrastructures, urbanisation, hydropower and mining projects. Of course, scholars are generally able to look beyond the beliefs, theories and facts they adhere to, and deal with contra-points that challenge their worldviews, but often we tend to collect and cherish those data and insights that confirm what we already believe. This is called *confirmation bias* in the psychological literature (Nickerson, 1998).

The above analysis raises the philosophical question of how these layers – beliefs, theories and facts – relate to one another (Crotty, 1998). Postmodernists and constructivists would argue that what we call 'facts' are strongly, if not fully, determined by our beliefs, theories and discourses. Hence, 'given' facts, independent of our social and scientific worldviews, do not exist; or at least, we do not have direct access to them. Positivists and empiricists argue the opposite; they claim that objective facts exist in the real world 'out there', independent from our beliefs and theories, and that we should allow objective facts to speak for themselves (through the scientific method as positivists and empiricists define it). However, this Element tries to find a middle road, inspired by philosophical pragmatism. This philosophy of science accepts various sources of knowledge: intelligence, culture *and* reality 'out there' (Bernstein, 2010). Hence, factual worlds as such do exist, but knowledge about them is strongly interwoven with our social and scientific worldviews. One cannot separate them, nor dissolve one into the other. So when this Element argues that the (implicit) worldviews of scholars, like Hydra and Chloris, play roles in assessing the performance of forest governance, this should not be misunderstood as the radical postmodernist claim that scientific knowledge lacks any reference point to distinguish fact from fiction, evidence from non-evidence and truth from falseness (although the pragmatist 'theory of truth' differs from the one of positivism; see Section 3). Hence, one can definitely believe in evidence-based policy and governance, like I do, but at the same time consider them in the context of scientific and societal worldviews. In Section 3 of this Element, these philosophical questions will be further elaborated.

All in all, this text aims to provide an academic, concise and accessible 'state-of-the-art' overview of forest governance and its performance (again, naturally from my own perspective). The following questions are addressed: How is forest governance defined (differently)? How has it responded to forest-related problems and opportunities? How has it evolved over time? What diverse policy ideas and institutional arrangements have emerged at national and international levels? Do these perform? And how will these ideas, arrangements and performances be interpreted from Chloris and Hydra worldviews?

To assess the performance of the various forest governance initiatives, I adopt the UN's Global Forest Goals (GFGs) as reference points (ECOSOC, 2017). The reason for doing so is that these goals have been adopted by the UN in New York in 2017, and hence, can be considered to be widely supported, policy relevant and socially legitimate. Six GFGs were agreed upon: (1) to reverse the loss of forest cover worldwide through SFM; (2) to enhance the socio-economic and environmental benefits from forests; (3) to significantly increase the area of protected forests; (4) to increase funding for SFM and research; (5) to promote forest governance frameworks that contribute to the Sustainable Development Goals (SDGs); and (6) to enhance cooperation, coordination and coherence among governments and with stakeholders. Now, for whether the forest governance initiatives that are dealt with in this Element, like FLEGT, REDD+, FC and PFM, contribute to achieving (parts of) one or more of these GFGs, these are assessed as 'performing' (how this performance will be measured and interpreted will be explained later).

2 Forest Governance: Setting the Scene

It seems trivial to formally define what a forest is, because everybody simply knows, right? A forest is a bunch of trees on a sufficiently large piece of land. Yet, it is not that simple. Compare for example tropical rainforests in Brazil with arid dry forests in the southern part of Ethiopia. Both are forests for locals, but Brazilians would hardly recognise a forest if they were dropped in Southern Ethiopia. On top of that, land with (rather) dense canopies can be very different things: a primary natural forest, a secondary managed forest, a restored forest, a reforested area, an afforested area, a multi-species or single-species plantation, a forested mosaic landscape and many more. No wonder that the FAO struggled to reach consensus over the last couple of decades. Currently, the following definition is used, which was agreed upon in the late 1990s:

> Forest includes natural forests and forest plantations. It is used to refer to land with a tree canopy cover of more than 10 percent and area of more than 0.5 ha. Forests are determined both by the presence of trees and the absence of other predominant land uses. The trees should be able to reach a minimum height of 5 m. Young stands that have not yet but are expected to reach a crown density of 10 percent and tree height of 5 m are included under forest, as are temporarily unstocked areas. The term includes forests used for purposes of production, protection, multiple-use or conservation (i.e. forest in national parks, nature reserves and other protected areas), as well as forest stands on agricultural lands (e.g. windbreaks and shelterbelts of trees with a width of more than 20 m), and rubberwood plantations and cork oak stands. The term specifically excludes stands of trees established primarily for agricultural production, for example fruit tree plantations. It also excludes trees planted in agroforestry systems. (FAO, 2000, Appendix 2)

The fact that this consensus definition was agreed upon in the late 1990s implies that the FAO operated with another one *before*. Then, a canopy cover of 20 per cent, a height of seven metres, and an area of 1.0 ha, was the minimum requirement to be labelled 'a forest', but this definition excluded forests like those in Southern Ethiopia, as well as forested mosaic landscapes. However, a change of definition obviously has consequences. Chazdon and colleagues (2016) note:

> For example, the estimate of global forest area increased by 300 million ha (approximately 10 %) between 1990 and 2000 simply because the FRA changed its global definition of forest, reducing the minimum height from 7 to 5 m, reducing the minimum area from 1.0 to 0.5 ha. and reducing minimum crown cover from 20 to 10 %. In Australia, where trees often occur in open vegetation formations, this reclassification led to the acquisition of an additional 118 million ha of forest.

Hence, definitions are not so trivial. In addition, by summing up all forest-like vegetation on a global scale, one does not distinguish between primary forests and plantations, for example. So, a recorded net increase of forests in a country can still parallel a decrease in natural forests, simply because the expansion of plantations overcompensates for the loss of primary forests. Nonetheless, with current GIS technologies and improved inventory methods on the ground, global forest assessments and national forest inventories have also gradually become more precise in categorisation and more accurate in spatial estimates (Chazdon et al., 2016).

Currently, the world's forest cover is recorded at just over 4 billion ha, which amounts to 31.1 per cent of global land area (FAO, 2020). Most is still designated as natural forest, whereas about one-third is production forest, which can be primary, secondary or plantation forests. About 18 per cent of the world's forests are located in legally established protected areas.

2.1 Forest Values

For scientists, definitions and data are crucially important; lay people, however, are generally more interested in values. For most people, the question is not so much what *is* a forest, but what it does *mean* for them in daily life? Environmental philosophers and ethicists generally distinguish three values that people hold for nature (and forests): (1) instrumental values; (2) intrinsic values; and (3) relational values (Himes and Muraca, 2018). Instrumental values are those that serve human interests and preferences, or more broadly, that enable people to survive or to live a good life (in a material sense). Examples from forests are timber, fruits, nuts, mushrooms, fuel wood, bush meat, fodder, water regulation, soil stability, micro climate, etc. What these different products and ecosystem services conceptually share is that they are all based on an *anthropocentric* perspective. The fundamental question is: What benefits does nature – or do forests – bring to people?

Intrinsic values are positioned at the other end of the continuum, hence, they are *ecocentric* in character. Forests, trees and forest biodiversity do have a value for *themselves*, independent of humans or human interests and benefits. If so, then they also have *a right to exist* for themselves, and cannot 'just' be appropriated by people for whatever reason. Philosophically, this is however a complex position, because it is still people that assign intrinsic values and non-human rights to nature and forests, so some scholars claim that such values and rights are difficult to formulate or grant (Justus et al., 2009). Others believe that people can still empathise with non-human species – cognitively, ethically and empathically – and thus identify values from nature's perspective.

Relational values, finally, are neither about humans or nature-in-itself, but about their *relationships* (Himes and Muraca, 2018). People can value these relationships very differently. Some go as far as claiming that they can literally communicate with nature; speaking with trees is, for example, a common practice for many. Others feel spiritual connections, informally and individually, or institutionally through religions. Again, others see these relationships more in rational and material terms, like attachment to specific places (respect for the place where they were born and for the landscape they live in) or in landscape art (so picturing nature's beauty, that brings value to both the art and the landscape).

2.2 Forest Issues

'Issues' are topics that generate substantial societal, political and/or media concern and, consequently, might be included in national and international policy agendas (Downs, 1972). Concerning forests, *the* current issue is deforestation (or in more 'neutral terms': the conversion of forest lands into other land use types). While writing this section, the human-induced, mostly illegal Amazon fires are again hot topics in worldwide social and traditional media, in relation to the weakening of Brazilian environmental policy by the Bolsonaro administration (October 2019).

Deforestation figures, however, differ. The most cited sources are the Global Forest Resources Assessments of the FAO, the latest being published in 2020. According to this report, there was an annual loss of about 11 million ha of forest area in the last decade – through forest clearing for other land uses, logging and natural disasters – and an annual gain of about 6 million ha – through afforestation, reforestation and natural regeneration – resulting in a net annual decrease in forest area of 4.7 million ha in the period 2010–20 (nearly the size of Costa Rica). Over the latest decades, this figure of net annual decrease has reduced significantly, from 7.8 million ha in the 1990s, to 5.2 million ha in the 2000s, to 4.7 million ha in the 2010s (FAO, 2020). However, this trend currently seems to be under pressure due to, for example, increasing rates of deforestation in the Amazon region (Butler, 2019).

These figures should be put into perspective though. The FAO's data and methods are criticised because these are dependent on voluntary country reporting and built upon the concept of 'forest area net change', which allows natural forest loss to be compensated for by forest plantations, for example, and which considers clear-cut areas that are supposed to be replanted as 'forest areas' too. Other scholars therefore use global data sets from satellite images and assess the change in forest *canopy* (not area). As a result, much higher deforestation rates are found, for example ~20 million ha annual global gross forest cover loss in 2000–5 (Hansen et al., 2010), compared to a gross annual decrease in forest area of ~12.9 million ha found by the FAO (2005). Greater still, Global Forest Watch, based on global satellite images analysis, estimates deforestation rates nine times that of the FAO in the 2010s, but these figures are also contested (Pearce, 2018). In contrast, others determined a net *increase* in tree cover in the period 1982–2016, resulting in a net annual gain of 6.6 million ha (Xiao-Peng et al., 2018). However, this increase does include net canopy *loss* in the tropics (about 18 million ha in the period 1982–2016), which is compensated for by a substantial increase in temperate and boreal forests. In short, definitions, methods, data and conclusions differ, but one thing is common across these studies: the occurrence of tropical deforestation.

Figures on deforestation include both man-made and natural causes, although this distinction is becoming increasingly problematic; for example, the recent massive forest fires in Australia, which were ignited by natural causes, such as thunderstorms, were subsequently fiercely accelerated by extreme drought and winds; conditions that are very likely related to human-induced climate change, so what is 'natural' about those? Geist and Lambin (2002) offer a framework to understand what they call proximate causes and underlying driving forces of tropical deforestation. The former (causes) are agricultural expansion (e.g. for livestock farming, soya production and palm oil plantations), infrastructure extension and wood extraction (besides natural causes); the latter (drivers) consist of economics, governance, technology, culture and demography. They conclude that it is wrong to adopt mono-causal explanations – like deforestation originates from slash-and-burn practices – but that multiple causes and drivers are nearly always at work, in different configurations in different regions. Also, some causes and drivers are more prominent than others, particularly extractive development models and commercial agricultural expansion. Their key conclusions about causes and drivers are still valid today (see for example Jayathilake et al., 2020), although a rise in small-scale deforestation occurrences, relative to large-scale forest clearances in Amazonia, have recently been observed, while new hotspots of deforestation are emerging in countries like Peru, Bolivia, Colombia and Congo DRC (Kalamandeen et al., 2018; Somorin, 2014).

Deforestation obviously produces many positive impacts, as it opens up 'lazy lands' for productive economic activities, such as agriculture, the timber industry, hydropower, mining, etc. (Soto Golcher, 2020). This is also the argument that many Brazilians (and others) use to counteract the conservationist tendencies in the West: 'These forest lands are ours and we need them for our economic development, just as you appropriated your domestic forests, as well as the forests in the colonies, in the past' (paraphrased from: Humphreys, 1996; Kolk, 1996). But, deforestation also exhibits several detrimental effects (Bosetti and Lubowski, 2010; Grainger, 2009; FAO, 2018b): (1) deterioration of local livelihoods (about one billion people worldwide directly depend on forest products and services for their daily survival); (2) loss of biodiversity (forests house about 80 per cent of the world's terrestrial biodiversity); (3) lost income from over-harvested and nearly-extinct valuable timber species (the global timber market value was about 225 billion dollars in 2016, so there is a lot to lose); (4) adverse effects on local climates, like droughts, erosion, landslides and flooding; and (5) accelerating human-induced global warming (about 15 per cent of current greenhouse gas emissions can be attributed to deforestation and forest degradation).

Besides deforestation, many other issues dominate current agendas, for example forest degradation, illegal logging, forest tenure, forest rights, food security, water management, forest conflicts, forest crime, etc., some of which I will return to in the rest of the Element (Hoogeveen and Verkooijen, 2010; Rayner et al., 2010). And since 2020, another topic has truly resonated in media and science: the global spread of new viruses connected to forests, deforestation and forest degradation, such as HIV, Ebola, SARS and most recently Covid-19 (Vidal, 2020).

2.3 Forest Policies

Traditional, but rather outdated, definitions of 'policy' only refer to governments: 'A policy is whatever governments choose to do or not do' (Birkland, 2005: 17). Hence, a forest policy covers everything a certain government does related to the forests in its territory, so activities of private actors – like companies or forest owners – are excluded. A policy is therefore a *public* thing, and particularly points at the design, implementation and monitoring of forest laws, plans, programmes, projects and funds as decided upon by the legislative branch – the parliament – of a democratic state (Van der Graaf and Hoppe, 1996).[1] Policies consists of various elements at different levels of abstraction (Cashore and Howlett, 2007; McDermott et al., 2010): ambitions, objectives, targets and timetables, means, instruments, settings, resources, courses of actions, etc. (many of which I will come back to in the rest of this Element). In forest policy, governmental ambitions often relate to sustainable forest management, a healthy forest sector with sufficient employment, profitable timber trade, recreation, biodiversity conservation and regulating conflicts among diverse forest interests (Krott, 2005; Umans, 1993; Wiersum, 1995).

More recent definitions of policy are, however, much broader and much more detailed in scope than the traditional ones, and go beyond its governmental and public natures per se. At the same time, they have also become more *modest* in nature, because the belief in top-down, *blue-print* planning of society and economy by a strong state has waned since the 1980s (Pierre, 2000). Some scholars still stay close to the traditional definition, for example: 'Policy is what *organizations* do' (Mayers and Bass, 2004: 39). Others claim that policy is

---

[1] Obviously, this works differently in an authoritarian state or dictatorship, in which the legislative, executive and judicial powers of the state are controlled by a few or even by one person.

omnipresent in current late-modern society (Abma and In 't Veld, 2001: 15). Today, even the planning of the family household may be called 'a policy'. Yet, I propose to limit the term policy to the *public realm*, like the traditional definition does, but nonetheless consider the *inclusion of private actors* in its description very helpful to analyse current policy issues. Particularly literature on policy networks, policy arrangements, policy discourses and advocacy coalitions does include private actors in their public policy definitions (Hajer and Wagenaar, 2003; Kickert et al., 1997; Mol et al., 2000; Sabatier, 2007; Van Tatenhove et al., 2000; Van Waarden, 1992). From these perspectives, a policy can be considered 'a joint initiative of public and private actors – in networks, arrangements, or coalitions – to discuss and address societal problems and opportunities'.

Generally, a policy is a response to 'an issue on the public agenda'. Hence, forest policies can be considered responses to the many forest issues previously identified, such as deforestation or illegal logging. However, the relationships between issues, agendas and policies are complex, as various scholars observe (Baumgarter et al., 2006; Dunn, 2016). The most straightforward theory, the *issue-attention cycle*, claims that public issues come and go, particularly through media attention (Downs, 1972). Other theories, such as the *multiple streams* approach, deem this picture far too simple, and claim that problems, policies and politics need to be actively linked by so-called policy entrepreneurs at the right time and in the right place (Kingdon, 2014). Others believe that agenda-setting occurs behind closed doors, invisible to the larger public, where key political interests and powers – the *old-boys networks* of this world – decide what can be subject to public policy, and what not (Bachrach and Baratz, 1962; Krott, 2005). It is nonetheless likely that all three – media, entrepreneurship and power – are important factors in agenda-setting and policy design.

2.4 Forest Governance[2]

The terms 'policy' and 'governance' are highly interlinked. One way of distinguishing them is relating policy to *what* and governance to *how*. Policy defines what we aim for on paper, governance how we might achieve those aims in practice. This also follows from the etymology of governance, *kúbernan*, the Greek word for 'piloting', 'steering' or 'directing' (Kjaer, 2004). One definition of governance therefore goes as follows: 'The capacity of government to make and implement policy – in other words, to steer society' (Pierre and Peters, 2000: 1). But this definition particularly refers to the state-centric conception of governance, or 'old' governance (Pierre, 2000). In contrast, the society-centric,

---

[2] This subsection includes text fragments from earlier work, particularly Arts (2014).

'new' governance alternative particularly focuses on the coordination of collective action by public and private actors to address societal problems and opportunities (based on: Hogl et al., 2012; Kooiman, 2003; Nye and Donahue, 2000; Pierre, 2000). Whereas, the governance mechanisms at work can take several forms: state, market, network or community. Some scholars also present definitions that integrate both the old and new governance interpretations, like Bevir (2012: 1): 'Governance refers ... to all processes of governing, whether undertaken by a government, market, or network, whether over a family, tribe, formal or informal organisation, or territory, and whether through laws, norms, power or language'.

To achieve certain policy aims, society – or parts of society – should be *directed*, *steered* or *governed* towards those aims, for example by changing people's individual behaviour (e.g. to get them to buy more healthy food) or by facilitating collective action (e.g. mobilising hospitals to work together to fight the Covid-19 crisis). However, as we all know, people or groups do not easily change their behaviour. Therefore, governments, governors, organisations or CEOs use certain 'techniques of governance' – also called 'policy instruments', to further complicate the distinction between policy and governance – to achieve such individual or social change. In the classical literature on policy instruments, a distinction is made between sticks, carrots, sermons and infrastructures – or regulatory, economic, communicative and physical instruments (Bemelmans-Videc et al., 2010; Hoogerwerf and Herwijer, 2008; Krott, 2005).

A 'stick' refers to coercion, simply to force people to change. A binding law with active policing and sanctioning is *the* exemplar of a stick. For example, a forest owner in the Netherlands is obliged to replant a tree after felling (although exceptions exist). A 'carrot' refers to reward, to persuade a target group to change its behaviour through incentives. A subsidy on electric cars is a good example, another is subsidies for farmers to consider the inclusion of nature conservation in their business model. A 'sermon' focuses on information dissemination or on ethics, so informing the public about certain issues, decisions and policies or trying to convince an audience to do things differently on moral grounds. Information or messages are communicated to certain target audiences, but are not backed by binding law and do not mobilise additional incentives, although they can refer to them, for example to increase public understanding of policy or to call upon citizens to improve their lifestyles. Finally, 'infrastructure'. This is best explained as 'crowd control'. At festivals or airports, crowds are steered by certain measures, such as gates, tunnels, passages, controllers, etc. In fact, governments do the same, but at the scale of entire territories. For example, they build or contribute to infrastructures of roads, canals, cameras, computers, green corridors, industrial sites, etc., to govern flows of people, nature, materials and information.

The above distinctions (stick, carrot, sermon, infrastructure) are referred to as the 'first generation of policy instruments' (Howlett, 2004). These are based on direct, substantive interventions of governments to produce or redistribute certain collective goods and services (like security, welfare, health, environmental quality, etc.). During recent decades, however, direct control of governments and *blue-print* planning – 'old' governance, so to speak – became less popular and less possible, so that a new, 'second generation of policy instruments' has emerged. These are more based on *indirect* control by governments and are more *procedural* than substantive in nature (although this does not mean that classical laws, incentives and campaigns have become obsolete). Therefore, some scholars associate this second generation of instruments more with governance than with policy (Van der Steen et al., 2018). Examples are market-based instruments such as forest certifications, fish quotas, payment for ecosystem services, carbon taxes and cap-and-trade systems, like the European Union's Emission Trading System (ETS) to mitigate carbon dioxide emissions; or new regulatory instruments such as covenants, public-private partnerships, green deals and voluntary commitments by industry, combined with obligatory forms of public accountability (Steurer, 2013).

Many scholars however believe that the sole focus on instruments is too limited to grasp and analyse old and new techniques of governance. They, for example, prefer to look at institutional arrangements *as a whole*. Take the following definition of forest governance by Giessen and Buttoud (2014): 'Forest governance refers to all formal and informal, public and private institutional arrangements, the social interactions therein, and the effects of these on forests'. This definition goes far beyond governments' policy instruments alone and also includes rules of the game (institutions), actors and coalitions (social interactions) and impacts (effects on forests). The reasoning is that instruments are always part of broader institutional contexts (like governments, markets, networks and/or communities), need to operate through groups of people and only come into being through their effects. Moreover, the definition also recognises the existence of classical approaches (public, formal governance) and newer ones (private, informal governance). Hence, these scholars prefer a broad and holistic analysis of the various modes of forest governance.

Whereas previous definitions refer to *all* modes of forest governance, Agrawal and colleagues (2008: 1460) cover *new* modes of governance in particular, like decentralisation and privatisation, which they express as follows: 'The move away from centrally administered, top-down regulatory forest policies that characterized much of forestry in the 19th and 20th centuries'. To refer to such 'moves away', other authors speak of 'governance without government' or 'a shift from government to governance' (Rhodes, 1996; Rosenau and Czempiel, 1992; Van Kersbergen and Van Waarden, 2004). The key idea is that societies are steered differently towards public aims, goods and services today than they were previously. Governments have withdrawn, been hollowed out, or reduced in size, as a consequence of criticism of central state planning, the rise of globalisation and the emergence of neo-liberalism and new public management (Dunleavy and Hood, 1994; Osborne and Gaebler, 1992; Pierre, 2000; Van Tatenhove et al., 2000).

Given the above discussion, Arnouts and colleagues (2012) distinguish two governance literatures: one on *modes* (various co-existing modes of governance) and one on *shifts* (new modes of governance only). I will use this distinction later in this Element as well, but add a third literature on governance *norms*. This last category is related to 'good governance', which is a term philosophically different from the previous ones in this section, since we now move from *description* to *prescription*, or from *rational analysis* to *normative interpretation* (Biermann and Pattberg, 2012; Dunn, 2016). Good governance refers to practices or reforms of the public sector and of corporate management in accordance with a number of normative criteria, such as cost-effectiveness, transparency, accountability and participation (Bevir, 2012; Kjaer, 2004; Woods, 2000). Good governance is, among others, advocated by the European Union (EU), the International Monetary Fund (IMF) and the World Bank. Examples of 'good governance' programmes are new public management (NPM), which applies business principles to public administration for improved cost-effectiveness (Osborne and Gaebler, 1992). Or corporate social responsibility (CSR), which applies principles of responsible government to business practices for improved accountability (Bendel, 2000). Such approaches are also applied in the forest sector, particularly advocated by the FAO and the World Bank (FAO-PROFOR, 2011). Here the term 'good forest governance' is in vogue.

2.5 International Forest Governance

Many forest and forest-related issues referred to previously are transboundary in nature or do have transboundary repercussions (timber trade, deforestation, biodiversity loss, climate change, illegal logging). Therefore, forest policy and governance do not restrict themselves to national territories. International initiatives are abundant; for example, Fernández-Blanco and colleagues (2019) distinguish forty-one 'institutional elements' in global forest (-related) governance, from declarations, agreements and global objectives to certification systems. But overall, international forest policy and governance are considered 'weak' (Dimitrov, 2005). First of all, this is related to the nature of international politics itself. A world government is lacking, so 'coercive sticks' are hardly available (Waltz, 1979). Of course, binding international law exists, but compared to national law, its status is much weaker, and sanctions for non-compliant behaviour by governments are often lacking. A source of coercion other than international law may be powerful states – or so-called benign hegemons – that are able and willing to force others to follow the international rule of law (Webb and Krasner, 1989). Such instances do indeed occur (the USA and its allies forcing the Iraqi Hussein regime out of power in the 2000s is a clear example), but they can also easily turn into the opposite: a 'malign hegemon' bullying the world for its own interests.[3]

The first reason of 'weakness' – the lack of a world government – applies to all international policymaking. But international forest policy adds other weaknesses on top of that. After all, trees are standing *within* national territories, unlike transboundary flows such as water and air, and the substances transported by them. Hence, certain countries simply *deny* the international dimension of forest issues, like Brazil, Indonesia and Malaysia, that very strongly oppose the tendency in the world to see their forests as 'global goods' (Humphreys, 1996; Kolk, 1996). In addition, international topics that are not primarily about war and security, or about economics and markets, are considered 'low politics', read *irrelevant* politics, according to many international relations scholars (Waltz, 1979). And forests are one of those. Finally, international forest policy and governance lacks teeth (Humphreys, 1996, 2006). A legally binding international forest convention, comparable to the UNFCCC (United Nations Framework Convention on Climate Change), CBD (Convention on Biological Diversity) and UNCCD (United Nations Convention to Combat Desertification), is lacking, despite several attempts to negotiate one. Hence, international forest policy is largely voluntary in nature. For example, an *International Arrangements on Forests* does exist – consisting of various elements, like the UN Forum on Forests (UNFF) and the UN Forest Strategy, including the six Global Forest Goals, earlier referred to – but the decisions and rules of this arrangement cannot be forced upon countries (Maguire, 2013; Sotirov et al., 2020). Exceptions are rules of those legally binding trade and environmental agreements that *relate* to forests and trees (for example

---

[3] A unique form of international governance is the European Union, given its *supranational* characteristics, meaning that a substantial part of its powers and laws supersede those of its member states (Knill and Liefferink, 2013). However, forests still belong to the national competency of member states, although these might be *related* to issues that *do* fall under EU competency, like trade and environment.

UNFCCC, CBD, International Tropical Timber Agreement and Convention on International Trade in Endangered Species of Wild Fauna and Flora). These do indeed affect forest governance within countries in various instances (e.g. the protection of forest biodiversity under the legally binding requirements of the CBD, or the legal prohibition of importing seeds of protected tree species under CITES).

A debate has emerged whether voluntary international forest policy and governance are to be considered symbolic initiatives only, or whether these can make a real difference on the ground (Arts and Babili, 2013; Giessen, 2013). This is a clear case for so-called neo-realists and many regime theorists: states rule the world, particularly on security, economic and trade issues, and all the rest is irrelevant, including forests (Dimitrov et al., 2007; Keohane, 1984; Waltz, 1979). Scholars presenting competing approaches, though, like global governance perspectives, disagree (Biermann, 2007; Biermann and Pattberg, 2012; Held and McGrew, 2002; Pattberg, 2007; Rosenau, 1988). They include non-state actors and so-called transnational relations – running from the local to the' global level, and back – in their analyses. They also see the relevance of broader international agendas, including the environment. And many are also convinced, based on empirical observations, that these international actors, relations and institutions are regularly consequential for forestry practices on the ground, irrespective of whether these are based on hard law (legally binding treaties) or soft law (voluntary instruments).

3 Analysing Forest Governance

Governance is a contested concept. Several definitions exist (Kjaer, 2004; Van Kersbergen and Van Waarden, 2004). In order to deal with this plurality, this Element distinguishes three governance literatures, as was already stated in the previous section: (1) governance *modes*, (2) governance *shifts* and (3) governance *norms*. Each comes with its own definitions, which will be elaborated in Sections 4 to 6 of the Element. But having definitions is one thing, employing a perspective is another. According to many philosophers of science, all research is *theory-laden*, because pure inductive research, without a priori theorising, either consciously or unconsciously, does not exist, so you better explicate your theoretical perspective and scientific worldview (Crotty, 1998). This Element does so in this section, and is inspired by *discursive institutionalism* on the one hand and *philosophical pragmatism* on the other. The first refers to theory, to the specific analysis of forest governance arrangements in this Element (Subsection 3.1); the second refers to epistemology, to the ways through which knowledge about forest governance was produced

(Subsection 3.2). Of course, both are – and should be – linked, which will be explained in the analytical framework below (Subsection 3.3). Since philosophical pragmatism asks for theoretical pluralism and critical reflection, both Chloris and Hydra worldviews will be addressed in this framework.

3.1 Discursive Institutionalism[4]

The theoretical perspective on which this Element is built is *discursive institutionalism* (or DI), drawing from earlier work (Arts and Buizer, 2009; Buijs et al., 2014; Den Besten et al., 2014), and from established theories in governance studies, notably institutionalism and discourse theory (Hajer and Wagenaar, 2003; Kjaer, 2004; Pierre and Peters, 2000; Rhodes, 1996). The former considers politics, policy and governance from the perspective of institutions (as the name already suggests). A famous definition of an institution is the one of Noble Prize winner Douglass North (1990: 3): 'Institutions are the rules of the game in a society or, more formally, are the humanly devised constraints that shape human interaction.' According to institutionalism, every social system exhibits, designs and revises rules that steer the behaviour of (groups of) people. Law is of course an obvious example, but governance may also be exercised through incentives, norms and words (see the discussion on policy instruments in the previous section). Today, most institutionalists consider themselves *neo-*institutionalists, implying the existence of a classical approach too (Hall and Taylor, 1996; Schmidt, 2005). The difference is that the *neos* put more emphasis on rules (besides organisations), informal institutions (besides formal ones) and dynamics (besides stability) than their classical peers. The perspective on governance from neo-institutionalism is that state steering or societal steering needs to be based on *institutional logics*, thus designing, maintaining or reforming norms, values, rules and procedures that people (tend to) follow, and that contribute to achieving public goods, or avoiding 'public bads' (Kjaer, 2004; Ostrom, 1990).

Discourse theory, the second building-block of DI, focuses on the power of language (Fischer, 2003; Van den Brink and Metze, 2007).[5] The common assumption is that texts, concepts, narratives, frames and epistemes matter in policy and governance and shape the identities, ideas, interests, institutions and

---

[4] This subsection includes text fragments from earlier work, particularly Arts and Buizer (2009) and Buijs and colleagues (2014).

[5] In Section 1, the concept of 'worldview' is introduced, consequently one may wonder how discourses and worldviews differ from one another. Well, worldviews are beliefs, theories and facts one adheres to, so these are cognitive in nature, and related to the individual mind. Discourses on the other hand are discursive and interactive in nature, and relate to language, communication and social interaction. Worldviews and discourses co-shape one another.

choices of political systems and agencies. Hence, language is not a neutral device, but produces certain realities, and not others. For example, discourse defines issues *into* or *outside* politics, through agenda-setting processes (Hajer, 1995). Two traditions can be distinguished in discourse theory: 'thin' and 'thick' (Arts et al., 2010; Hay, 2002). The first considers discourse as ideas, arguments, framings and communicative devices that exist *besides* practices, institutions, structures and things (Dryzek, 2005; Habermas, 1996; Schmidt, 2008). So, language and interpretations *as opposed to* social and material objects and facts. Many scholars favour such 'analytical dualism' in order to make causal inferences, for example how discourses influence human behaviour and social institutions, and the other way around (Archer, 1996; Schmidt, 2008).

The 'thick' tradition, however, fuses discourses, social practices and materialities at the theoretical level, because these entities are considered fundamentally relational and intertwined. This is visible in Hajer's (1995: 44) definition, probably the most cited one in the literature: 'A discourse is a specific ensemble of ideas, concepts, and categorizations that are produced, reproduced and transformed in a particular set of practices and through which meaning is given to physical and social realities.' With this definition, Hajer stands in the Foucauldian tradition (although he also adds insights from argumentative theory to his analysis). For Foucault (2002), societal and scientific discourses – for example on sexuality, health or economy – define what subject identities, social practices and governance technologies are acceptable in a society, and which ones are not. This 'thick' conceptualisation of discourse *includes* social and material realities, and so goes far beyond only communicative devices. Besides, relationships are not considered causal here, but *emergent*, because discourses and realities co-emerge *simultaneously*.

Coming back to *discursive institutionalism*, DI can first of all be considered a new branch in neo-institutionalism (Blyth, 2002; Hay, 2006; Phillips et al., 2004; Schmidt, 2008). It tries to overcome some of the 'orthodoxies' in institutional thinking, like path-dependency and institutional breakdown. The former concept particularly addresses stability, continuity or even inertness in social orders through established institutional arrangements, whereas the latter concept refers to situations in which a given institutional order cannot cope with a crisis, leading to its breakdown (Peters et al., 2005). Now DI adds the concept of 'path shaping' – that refers to gradual transformation *without* immediate breakdowns – to the one of path-dependency (Hay, 2006; Streeck and Thelen, 2005). In understanding such path formations, discursive institutionalism emphasises the role of new, emerging ideas and discourses that undermine or reshape existing institutional arrangements, particularly when the latter are under social or economic pressure, and are losing credibility and legitimacy (Buijs et al., 2014). An example is the shift from Keynesian to monetarist economics, when the 'big' European welfare states received increasing criticism in the 1980s (Schmidt, 2008). In doing so, DI bridges the gap between institutional theory and discourse theory (Arts and Buizer, 2009). It brings in new dynamics and discursive understandings in institutional thinking and also helps discourse theory to go beyond mere ideas, frames and communicative devices, and also includes institutionalisation processes in the approach.

Analytically, DI makes a clear distinction between discourses and institutions to position itself in the 'thin' tradition of discourse theory. To visualise this point of departure, Den Besten and colleagues (2014) introduced the so-called discursive-institutional spiral in which new ideas and actors force discursive responses and institutional changes in subsequent rounds of public deliberation and policymaking. Generally, discourses in DI are seen as shared – and at the same time contested – ideas about social and material worlds in communicative devices (texts, speeches, narratives, etc.), and institutions as anchored ideas in formal and informal regulatory arrangements (laws, rules, norms, standards, procedures, etc., both on paper and in use) (Arts and Buizer, 2009; Habermas, 1996; Schmidt, 2008). With such 'analytical dualism' (Archer, 1996), discursive institutionalism departs from 'thick' discourse theory that emphasises the unity of 'the ideational' and 'the material' in discursive regimes (Foucault, 1971, 2002; Hajer, 1995). In addition, it puts much more emphasis on the *interactive* part of discourse formation and hence on the intervening role of 'agency' in discursive-institutional dynamics (Leipold and Winkler, 2017).

When talking about (forest) governance discourses in this Element, these relate to *both* science and policy. Academic scholars contribute to how we define and conceptualise the idea of governance, but policymakers do so as well, through designing and implementing policies in practice. A governance discourse is therefore neither purely scientific nor purely societal, but always hybrid.

3.2 Philosophical Pragmatism

Discursive institutionalism implies *theoretical pluralism*, a combination of theories, an approach which is epistemologically defended by philosophical pragmatism (Bohman, 1999). Moreover, the latter also advocates *mixed methods* (Tashakkori and Teddlie, 2010), an approach by which this work is also inspired (and which will be explained below). It is no surprise that pragmatism was therefore chosen as *the* epistemological foundation for this Element. Emerging in the USA in the nineteenth century, pragmatism was a response to European philosophy at that time, particularly the divide between idealism and empiricism, a schism which pragmatists did not find very productive (Bernstein, 2010). The most famous founders were Charles Sander Peirce, William James and John Dewey. Later, pragmatism co-evolved with analytical philosophy, critical theory and the linguistic turn in the twentieth century, through scholars such as Haack, Habermas, Putnam and Rorty. Such broad engagements with so many schools of thought already indicate that pragmatism does not represent one consistent philosophical system. Rather, it is 'a method of reflection' and a 'series of theses' on several epistemological questions, that often run counter to mainstream philosophy (Crotty, 1998; Keulartz et al., 2004).

A first characteristic that pragmatists nonetheless unite under is their quest for *via media* – for middle-ways or syntheses – among extremes, in order to overcome various dualisms of modern philosophy, such as subject and object, absolutism and relativism, rationalism and empiricism, positivism and constructivism,[6] as well as facts and values (Bernstein, 2010; Cochran, 2002; Legg, 2008). In so doing, they have refused to choose for one school or the other and defended the thesis that knowledge production comes from various sources: *subjectivism* (mind, thought, ratio, logic), *objectivism* (experience, observation, measurement, data) and *intersubjectivity* (language, argumentation, deliberation, culture). Whereas rationalists emphasise the first, empiricists the second and constructivists the third, pragmatism embraces *all* at the same time, yet without isolating one from the other, or absolutising one over the other. Nonetheless, they have developed their own theses regarding those knowledge sources and their relationships.[7]

Firstly, rationality is, according to pragmatists, a crucial but *limited* source of knowledge, because other human characteristics than reason – such as faith, belief or emotions – are determinants of knowledge production on the world too (Bernstein, 2010). Consequently, pragmatists prefer the notion of 'intelligence' over 'rationality'. Secondly, objects and data do *not* speak for themselves, which some pragmatists refer to as 'The Myth of the Given', because we lack a direct, immediate access to reality. Since language, symbols and signs – so

---

[6] According to Crotty (1998), positivism cannot be confronted with constructivism, because the former is a methodology, the latter an epistemology, so one is comparing apples and pears. Even more so, the better term is *contructionism*, says Crotty (because for him, constructivism equates to subjectivism). However, in daily academic language, uttered by non-philosophers, the two are often presented as opposites. Whereas the first emphasises objective fact-finding through observation and experimentation as the basis of truth, the second emphasises the social nature of knowledge production and the social construction of truth claims (in the plural).

[7] Of course, individual pragmatists have had fierce debates on many of those issues among themselves too.

culture – are always in-between subjects and objects, the latter cannot escape human interpretation for scientific understanding and explanation. Thirdly, although pragmatists do not believe in *the* Truth, with a capital 'T', truth is definitely *more* than a belief or a social construction. To address this fundamental issue of science, pragmatists have developed their own theories of truth (Capps, 2019). They assume that truth is dependent on practice, to the degree that 'knowledge works effectively' in social practices. And many of them also strongly believe in open-ended deliberation, agreement and justification in the scientific community, or even in the social community as a whole, to arrive at valid truth claims. With the disclaimer that any such claim is always fallible, and therefore needs to be challenged and tested continuously.

Besides the search for *via media,* to avoid false dualisms, and besides a fallibilistic notion of science and truth, pragmatism is also characterised by 'pluralism' and 'a primacy of practice' (Bernstein, 2010; Bohman, 1999; Cochran, 2002; Legg, 2008). Pragmatism does not prescribe or prefer a single theory or methodology, as many philosophical schools or systems do, but believes in the critical engagement with a plurality of theories and with a mix of methodologies in inquiry and science, both quantitative and qualitative, and both data-driven (inductive) and theory-inspired (deductive).[8] Because nobody holds *the* universal and everlasting truth of a phenomenon, a variety of perspectives, methods and techniques can help to approach a research problem from various angles, and foster reflection, doubt and debate towards a more robust and generally accepted truth claim. Next, the 'primacy of practice' is expressed in the word 'pragmatism' itself. *Pragma* in Greek means 'deed'; hence, research needs to be action-oriented in its performance and in its results. Tashakkori and Teddlie (1998) even speak of the 'dictatorship of the research question'; so real-world research problems need, according to them, to be the key entry point of research, not theory or method. However, this focus on practice does not imply any animosity against theory. Theories are important for pragmatists too, however as *means,* or tools, for better understanding and solving actual problems and for addressing philosophical puzzles, but not as ends-for-themselves. This is also referred to as 'instrumentalism' (Bernstein, 2010).

Given the above characteristics, pragmatism runs the danger of being considered (too) 'instrumentalist', 'conformist' or 'non-critical'. Proctor therefore writes (1998: 367): 'By not defining itself carefully, philosophical pragmatism slips over to methodological pragmatism, which itself slips over to vulgar pragmatism in its lesser moments. Pragmatism as such lacks ... a "critical rhetoric"'. However, others argue that pragmatism *does* include critical

---

[8] Several pragmatists call this combination *abduction.*

reflection, for example through its fallibilistic notion of science, its pluralism in theory and method, its focus on practice and its critique on dualisms in philosophy (Bohman, 1999; Midtgarden, 2012). The reason that this critical dimension of pragmatism has been underacknowledged in the philosophical literature might be found in its 'utilitarian interpretation' by several European scholars (Crotty, 1998; Kadlec, 2006). They unjustifiably believed that pragmatism only offered a superficial, scientific interpretation of American capitalism, thus confirming the status quo in society.

3.3 Analytical Framework

Because philosophical pragmatism allows for theoretical and methodological pluralism while urging critical reflection, it offers an excellent basis for this Element. Indeed, several theories are combined to build a discursive-institutional framework. At the same time, in order to foster critical reflection, this DI framework will be challenged by alternative, critical theories in the various empirical sections to come. All this works in *five* steps. *Firstly*, three governance literatures on (forest) governance will be distinguished, as was already previously stated: (1) governance *modes*, (2) governance *shifts* and (3) governance *norms*. This categorisation is based on two distinctions often made in the literature: between 'modes' and 'shifts' on the one hand, and between 'analysis of governance' and 'good governance' on the other (see and compare: Arnouts et al., 2012; Arts, 2014; Bevir, 2012; Biermann and Pattberg, 2012; Pierre, 2000; Pierre and Peters, 2000; Rhodes, 1996; Van Kersbergen and Van Waarden, 2004; Woods, 2000). *Modes* refer to various arrangements among public and private actors to co-govern societal problems or opportunities; *shifts* include relocations of regulatory authority from public to private actors, implying self-governance arrangements; and *norms* refer to guidelines and criteria for good governance, for example for more effective, accountable and participatory governance arrangements.

Secondly, various governance discourses will be identified in the empirical sections to come. For example, in Section 4, I will make a distinction between 'early' and 'late-modern' governance; in Section 5, I identify 'governance without government' and 'experimentalist governance', and in Section 6, I distinguish between 'bad', 'good' and 'good enough governance'. I call these governance *discourses* – and not governance theories or governance approaches, for example – because these will be analysed through the lens of DI in the rest of the Element.

Thirdly, I will analyse the institutionalisation of these discourses in governance arrangements, in accordance with DI. I will do so through various case studies on Forest Sector Governance (FSG), Forest Law Enforcement, Governance and Trade (FLEGT), Reducing Emissions from Deforestation and Forest Degradation (REDD+), Forest Certification (FC) and Participatory Forest Management (PFM). These cases were chosen because they represent specific institutionalisations of the various governance discourses, and because of available data and earlier findings from my own and colleagues' research.[9]

Of particular interest, because of my pragmatist and discursive-institutional starting-points, is whether these (new) forest governance arrangements *perform in practice*, in other words, produce positive impacts for forests and people, and so contribute to attaining the Global Forest Objectives (GFGs, see Section 1). In order to assess such impacts, *fourthly*, I apply mixed methods, as advocated by pragmatist epistemology. I build on my own and others' qualitative data and methods, such as in-depth interviews, field observations and participation in forest governance practices, as well as on others' quantitative data and methods, such as household surveys, GIS data, ecological monitoring and quasi-experiments.

Finally, I reflect upon the discursive institutional analyses of forest governance by confronting those with critical theory in each empirical section (although I can only do so briefly). Often, governance scholars, including myself, tend to develop rather positive attitudes towards (new) governance potentialities and capacities ('what's in a name ... '). They generally believe that these will bring more effective and legitimate arrangements than traditional governmental approaches do. This of course relates to the worldview of Chloris, as introduced in Section 1. Yet, Hydra is present in the literature too, although its advocates generally use other concepts than governance to utter their criticisms (which is logical, otherwise one remains trapped in the governance vocabulary). Critical theories which are dealt with in the rest of the Element are 'political economy' (Section 4), 'neo-liberalisation' (Section 5) and 'governmentality' (Section 6). These have common qualities in that they challenge forest governance assumptions, capacities and performances. Table 2 summarises the analytical framework as elucidated in this subsection.

4 Governance Modes

This section elaborates upon the first governance literature, namely *governance modes*. It does so by introducing the 'governance triangle' and by identifying 'early' and 'late' modern governance. The focus is very much on the state, as key regulator, but actors from the market and civil society come into play as

---

[9] A large part of the empirical findings in this book are retrieved from my own research and from colleagues' studies which I (co)supervised. This explains the many self-citations.

Table 2 Analytical framework (based on discursive-institutionalism and philosophical pragmatism)

Step 1	Identification of three governance literatures, as derived from scholarly work (modes, shifts, norms)
Step 2	Identification of several governance discourses in these three literatures (from early-modern governance to experimentalist governance to good governance and others)
Step 3	Institutionalisation of these discourses in various forest governance arrangements (five case studies: FSG, FLEGT, FC, REDD+, PFM)
Step 4	Performance of these forest governance arrangements in practice (impact assessments through mixed methods)
Step 5	Critical reflection on discursive-institutional analyses of forest governance (political economy, neo-liberalisation, governmentality)

well. The way in which this occurs, however, differs substantially and substantively between the early and late phase. Whereas the former state-market-society relationships can be roughly typified as statism, neo-corporatism or pluralism, the latter is more often expressed in terms of complex networks, multi-level governance arrangements, public-private partnerships, and the like. It will be shown below how these two modernist governance discourses have been institutionalised in practice. The early-modern type is illustrated by 'forest sector governance' in Europe after World War II, and late-modern governance by the so-called FLEGT initiative of the EU from 2003 (which stands for Forest Law Enforcement, Governance and Trade).

4.1 The Governance Triangle

Governance 'in its broadest sense' can be best explained by the so-called governance triangle: the triangle of state (or government), market (or business) and civil society (or community), as well as their mutual relationships. This triangle is readily used in the scholarly governance literature, including forest governance (see for example: Abbott and Snidal, 2009; Arts, 2014; Lemos and Agrawal, 2006; Steurer, 2013; Van Tatenhove et al., 2000). An example is shown in Figure 3. It illustrates how these domains are linked, or can be linked, through public-private partnerships (for example, to finance infrastructural projects by ministries and companies), co-management (to jointly manage forests more effectively by state departments and community organisations) or voluntary standards (to make value chains more sustainable through

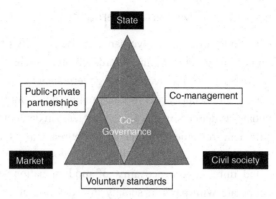

Figure 3 The governance triangle

standard-setting by trade organisations and NGOs). The overarching term of these phenomena is *co-governance*, to refer to joint governance initiatives by public and private actors (Arnouts et al., 2012). Nonetheless, the state is nearly always positioned at the top of the triangle by those scholars, so the starting point of analysis is generally 'governance *by* the state'. However, it also shows how the state is, or can be, related to the other two domains, and then it is all about 'governance *with* the state'.

Below, 'modern' and 'late-modern' governance will be distinguished in Subsections 4.2 and 4.4, respectively. The first refers to modern state regulation, as developed in European welfare states since World War II. During this period, state bureaucracies generally increased in size and covered more and more areas of social and economic life, including forests. This trend has largely reversed since the late 1980s and early 1990s, due to the reform of the welfare state, the emergence of monetarist economics and neo-liberal politics, the fall of the Berlin Wall and the rise of the global network society (Castells, 2000; Pierre, 2000; Schmidt, 2002; Van Tatenhove et al., 2000; Waters, 1995). Consequently, state bureaucracies were substantially downsized, while public policies and laws were reformed. Parallel, new co-governance arrangements gained popularity, although this has not excluded state or hierarchical regulation (Arnouts et al., 2012; Kooiman, 2003; Mol et al., 2000). Scholars have typified this turning point in different terms, such as the end of history, the shift from modernism to postmodernism, the rise of reflexive modernisation, the transition from first to second modernity, the shift from government to governance, new public management and neo-liberalism (Arts et al., 2009; Beck et al., 1994; Dunleavy and Hood, 1994; Fukuyama, 1989; Lyotard, 1984; Osborne and Gaebler, 1992). Here, I prefer to use the terminology 'early' and 'late' modernity (Van Tatenhove et al., 2000), which expresses a 'transformation' of governance rather than a 'radical rupture' of it, as compared to other terms, like postmodernism or second modernity.

4.2 Modern Governance

In 'early' modernist interpretations, governance is 'the capacity of government to make and implement policy, in other words, to steer society' (Pierre and Peters, 2000: 1; see Section 2). Governments govern societies in order to: (1) guarantee law, order and security, (2) produce public goods and services, (3) achieve public goals, as defined by that society (at least in democratic systems) and (4) tax sufficient revenues to finance its bureaucracies and policies (Hoogerwerf and Herwijer, 2008). A healthy forestry sector is generally part of the second and third governance aims of modern nation states. Often, governments cooperate with parts of society in order to realise these public goals, goods and services, or leave certain public duties to be executed by the private sector. In European comparative politics, three state-market-society relationships are generally distinguished in the governance triangle: statism, neo-corporatism and pluralism (Frouws, 1994; Hay et al., 2006; Pierre and Peters, 2000; Van Tatenhove et al., 2000; Van Waarden, 1992).

As the word itself expresses, *statism* is a system in which the state has a prominent and dominant role in public affairs, while it has the ambition to directly represent all societal interests in regulating the common good. The size of the state bureaucracy is generally substantial, if not large, and citizens enjoy extensive social arrangements during their life (childcare, education, health care, social welfare, pensions, etc.). In addition, markets are strongly regulated, or even partially nationalised, in order to guarantee or maintain the production of crucial goods and services, such as food, timber and steel, even against external market competition pressures. This sounds rather ideal, but statism has its flipside. It generally goes together with high tax pressures on population and industry, negative externalities of large bureaucracies, and economic ineffi-ciencies in state-regulated production sectors. Therefore, the (expensive) social arrangements can generally hardly be maintained over time, or only at the cost of high state budget deficits. Moreover, private affairs of citizens may be penetrated by state control in ways that humans find undesirable.

Pluralism is the counterpoint of statism. The state is much smaller in size, does not directly interfere in the private sector and only focuses on crucial aspects of public regulation (particularly law, order and security and strategic economic sectors, like energy). Interest groups, both from the market and civil society, play prominent roles in common affairs. Public policy is the result of negotiation and consensus seeking among plural interests, while the production of social arrangements and public goods may be outsourced to private parties, for example health care or pensions. Whereas this system is definitely much better able to avoid problems of bureaucracy and state intrusion, (parts of) social security arrangements become dependent on capricious market forces. For example, prices for public services may become too high for the poorer social classes in society.

Finally, *corporatism* sits in-between statism and pluralism. The state and the market may act like one body, or one 'corps', in certain sectors in order to align capital and labour in those sectors, and to avoid class conflict under state guidance. Traditionally, corporatism focuses on state-regulated wage negotiations among labour unions and employers' organisations. Once an agreement is settled, it is valid for the entire sector. *Neo*-corporatism refers to broader modes of cooperation among the state and the market. An example is agriculture or forestry in many European countries. The respective private sectors work intensively together with the relevant silos of the state bureaucracy. They jointly regulate relevant public affairs related to that sector, while also furthering the private interests at the same time. Societal organisations are even allowed to tax their own members on behalf of the state under (neo)corporatism in many instances. This system may suffer from similar disadvantages to statism, but 'sector-specific' in this case. It may also lead to unequal market relations, as some sectors are protected by intense state interventions, while others are not.

In literature, Central and Eastern European countries are generally considered statist, Northern and Western European countries neo-corporatist and the UK (and USA) pluralist (see for example Lenschow et al., 2005: 811). Of course, this picture is a caricature and does not do justice to the specifics of individual countries and of individual economic sectors. Moreover, the many European countries' systems have also substantially converged under the influence of the EU and have all been affected by globalisation and neo-liberalism, although differently in scope and size in each country and sector. Yet, the classification helps us to understand the ways in which the forest sectors have been governed in various countries, and how this governance system has changed over time.

4.3 Case I: 'Forest Sector Governance'[10]

Forest sector governance is about national-level sectoral policymaking and implementation within the confines of the modern nation state (Pierre, 2000, speaks of 'old' governance; see Section 2). This model has a long history, but still exists today, although under the pressure of several change processes (see Subsection 4.4). However, forests have been the object of state regulation since the Middle Ages (Umans, 1993). The nobilities in power wished to conserve hunting grounds, gazetted parts of the lands and forests for this purpose and thus

---

[10] This subsection includes text fragments from earlier work, particularly Arts (2014).

excluded ordinary people from entering them to harvest timber and non-timber forest products. In parallel, private and communal forests existed side-by-side in most areas, and these were used for personal gain and provision of local livelihoods, respectively (Jeanrenaud, 2001). In addition, large natural forest areas were found in 'no one's lands' everywhere in Europe, hardly impacted by people.

Later, with the birth of the modern state system in the seventeenth century, many forests were nationalised and state forests in particular were set aside and managed for 'public' timber production, for example to provide the navy and the water sector with enough strategic resources. As important, or even more important, according to Scott (1998), the state's interests in forests had a fiscal background as well, to produce sufficient revenues for the treasury. With this 'fiscal forestry', the focus increasingly shifted from forests as habitats with many species, functions and local uses, to monofunctional systems to produce timber, profits and revenues for the state and the market, further depriving local communities of 'their' forest resources. This focus was subsequently deepened with the emergence of 'scientific forestry' in German, France and later the USA in the eighteenth-century, to maximise timber production. Forests became entirely dismantled from their naturalness and began to look like monocultural croplands. Initial production figures were staggering, but figures in subsequent rotation cycles fell due to – primarily – the depletion of soils (Scott, 1998). In the meantime, harvesting in natural forests continued and expanded.

In the late seventeenth to early eighteenth centuries, the depletion of forest resources became paramount and critical in all ownership categories in Europe (state, private, communal). It was at that time that pioneers in forestry – such as the German Hans Carl von Carlowitz (1645–1714) – invented the notion of 'sustainability'. The idea of the sustainable yield introduced the concept that harvest from forests is brought into balance with its increment through the principles of scientific management (Grober, 2012). It took a century or so for this notion to mature and become practical in forestry. Soon after, nation states started to issue forest laws to enforce this sustainability principle – or variants thereof – and related management practices upon forest owners and users, an example of which is Belgium in 1847. It is from this era – around the mid-nineteenth century – onwards that forests in European states started to recover and expand again, after centuries of deforestation and degradation, although problems of depletion continued – and even increased in severity – in the colonies overseas (Vandergeest and Peluso, 2006).

Forest laws have probably remained the key policy instrument for modern states to govern their forest sectors. These laws generally stipulate topics like forest tenure, the size of allowable clear-cuts in forests, the obligation to reforest such clear-cuts, the key management principles of a country, the obligation for forest owners and managers to harvest timber sustainably, and the situations in which permits and concessions for forest operations are required (Agrawal et al., 2008; Krott, 2005; McDermott et al., 2010). Also, additional voluntary measures may be formulated in policy programmes, such as expansion of forest cover, protection of forest biodiversity, enhancement of forest beauty for recreation and fostering nature education in forests. Today, many countries around the world have adopted so-called National Forest Programmes (NFPs), in addition to their forest laws, in which the principles of Sustainable Forest Management (SFM) have been expanded into a range of policy measures related to economy, ecology and society (the three pillars of SFM) (FAO, 2015; Schanz, 2002). Besides laws ('sticks') and programmes ('sermons'), economic instruments ('carrots') have been overly used in the forest sector too. One may think of subsidies for commercial, fast-growing species, for laying out plantations, for opening forests to visitors or for protecting certain tree species or forest habitats.

Given certain state-society relationships, as elucidated in Subsection 4.2, the forest sector exercises more or less influence on state regulation. In pluralist or neo-corporatist arrangements, the private sector probably has more direct impact on policies, governance and instrument choices than in statist systems. Also, different instrument choices and implementation styles are prioritised in these arrangements: statist systems prefer top-down regulatory styles in forestry (France, Germany), pluralist ones bottom-up market-based or community-based approaches (UK), and neo-corporatist ones prioritise mixed styles (Scandinavia) (Sergent et al., 2018). In the Netherlands, for example, although not a typical forestry economy, until recently the private forest sector always had a big say in forest policy design and instrument choice (Den Ouden and Muys, 2010; Mohren and Vodde, 2006; Veenman et al., 2006). This is strongly related to the neo-corporatist structure of the Dutch forest sector after World War II. Through the Bosschap – the core association of employers, employees and public administrators in the forest sector at that time – the private sector was directly involved in state regulation, and policies and instruments were tailor-made to match the sector's private and public interests. Early-modern Dutch forest governance was also quite successful during those years: the forest area substantially expanded and multifunctional forestry became – slowly but surely – institutionalised as the mainstream approach in the sector, although critics have argued time and again that the layout of exotic, even-aged monocultures was far too dominant in the history of Dutch forestry, which went together with the loss of natural forests and native trees. In 2015, the Bosschap was annulled as one of the expressions of the shift from neo-corporatism to neo-liberalism in the

Netherlands, and new emphases (natural regeneration, nature protection, recreation) and new modes of governance (decentralisation, privatisation) have been introduced in the Dutch forestry sector. As a consequence, Dutch forest policy and law became increasingly integrated in nature conservation policy and law, as well as much more dependent on subnational and voluntary initiatives since the 1990s. Recently, though, a new sector-specific forest strategy was introduced in the Netherlands (LNV, 2020). New ambitions for forest expansion, climate-smart forest management, revitalisation of forests and the greening of cities and the countryside were formulated, but whether these will truly materialise in the coming decade is still an open question.

4.4 The Chloris of late-modern governance

In the late 1980s and early 1990s, as previously indicated, some drastic changes occurred: 1. the restructuring of the welfare state; 2. the fall of the Berlin Wall and the Soviet Union; and 3. the deepening of globalisation processes (Castells, 2000; Pierre, 2000; Van Tatenhove et al., 2000; Waters, 1995). The 1980s also confronted Western states with economic crises: the decline of primary industries, high unemployment rates and increasing inflation. Many experts accused Keynesian economics and welfare state politics of being the main causes of the problems, because these were said to go together with inefficient bureaucracies, public budget deficits and monetary depreciation. Monetarist economics and neo-liberal politics emerged as competitors of the dominant paradigms; first as ideas and discourses, then as early practices in Reaganomics and Thatcherism, and as institutionalised mainstreams thereafter (following discursive-institutional dynamics; Den Besten et al., 2014; Schmidt, 2002). These schools advocated a smaller and 'smart' state, a slimmed public budget with limited deficits, in combination with free trade, private liberty and self-regulation. Often, this is labelled 'New Public Management', or NPM (Dunleavy and Hood, 1994; Osborne and Gaebler, 1992).

At the same time, the Soviet Union imploded as a consequence of Gorbachev's perestroika and glasnost, and of Western economic and military hegemony. After which, Fukuyama (1989) labelled the world's new situation as 'the end of history', since liberalism had in his view overthrown all competing ideologies, particularly communism. The then US President Bush Sr declared that we faced a 'New World Order', in which liberal values, global trade, arms control, international cooperation and human rights had become – and should become – dominant everywhere (Miller and Yetiv, 2001). The belief in 'doing politics otherwise' inspired many. State bureaucracies were downsized, streamlined, partly privatised and made much more efficient, while several public tasks and duties were outsourced to subnational authorities, markets and communities, which were supposed to deal with those issues much more effectively and legitimately. The slimmed, national state now started 'to control at a distance'. At the same time, global governance emerged as a concept, the idea that states need to increase their international cooperation to address transboundary issues and problems, which was of course also enabled by the fall of the Berlin Wall and the 'New World Order' (Held and McGrew, 2002; Nye and Donahue, 2000). Through such worldwide governance changes, a more complex, multi-actor and multilevel system of regulation emerged in the 1990s, for which states and non-states were believed to be co-responsible. This is what we call 'late-modern' governance (Van Tatenhove et al., 2000).

This 'late' phase of governance engendered innovative structures and styles of regulation, compared to the 'early' statist, corporatist or pluralist regimes (although it would be a misunderstanding to believe that these old structures just evaporated; they continued to exist, but transformed towards the demands of the second phase at the same time; see Arts et al., 2009; Pierre, 2000). States and non-states now started to co-govern several issues through hybrid networks and arrangements, whereas second-generation instruments emerged (Howlett, 2004; Kooiman, 2003; Lemos and Agrawal, 2006; Mol et al., 2000; Steurer, 2013; Van Waarden, 1992). Examples are innovations in school education, co-management of natural resources, public-private partnerships in building energy infrastructures, agroecological schemes by farmers, facilitated by public authorities, and transboundary river-basin management as co-responsibility of governments and private stakeholders. The key feature of all those arrangements is *co-governance* among public and private actors in order to regulate specific issue arenas, while new instruments are often tried to foster public-private collaboration, stakeholder participation and regulatory innovation: for example walk-in evenings in city halls, deliberative fora, joint fact-finding meetings, start-ups of universities and companies, citizens' assemblies to inform governments, collaborative design shops, focus groups, serious games, living labs and so on. Often, these new structures and styles are considered progress in regulation, or are evaluated positively in the scholarly literature, in that they do potentially increase both performance and legitimacy of governance processes (which I like to refer to as the Chloris of late-modern governance) (Biermann and Gupta, 2011; Hogl et al., 2012; Van Kersbergen and Van Waarden, 2004).

4.5 Case II: Forest Law Enforcement, Governance and Trade

Forest Law Enforcement, Governance and Trade (FLEGT) is an action plan of the EU from 2003, implemented in collaboration with a group of timber-exporting countries, in order to combat illegal logging and illegal timber trade. To do so, the action plan encourages legal reform, forest governance reform, stakeholder participation and sustainable development in the forest sector through so-called Voluntary Partnership Agreements (VPAs). Currently, the following VPA-countries are involved: Cameroon, Central African Republic, Democratic Republic of Congo (DRC), Gabon, Ghana, Guyana, Honduras, Indonesia, Ivory Coast, Laos, Liberia, Malaysia, Republic of the Congo, Thailand and Vietnam (Nathan et al., 2014; www.euflegt.efi.int/home). Some countries are still negotiating an agreement with the EU (such as DRC and Laos); only one already exports FLEGT-licenced timber to the EU (Indonesia); and most other countries are somewhere in the middle, amid the implementation process.

Forest Law Enforcement, Governance and Trade exhibits many characteristics of a co-governance arrangement. It includes a so-called Voluntary Partnership Agreement (VPA) between the EU and each timber exporting country; the instalment of a Legality Assurance System (LAS) in each country (including a traceability system to follow legally sourced timber throughout the value chain); legal reform to converge national law with (inter)national legality standards; stakeholder participation in the entire FLEGT process (including timber companies, NGOs and local communities); a system for monitoring, review and verification of implementation and compliance (including independent third party audits); and a licencing system to label FLEGT timber for legal export, legal import and recognition of legality in markets.

On the EU side, the EU Timber Regulation (EUTR) was adopted in 2013 (Derous and Verhaeghe, 2019). It prohibits operators in the EU market from importing, trading or processing illegal timber or products thereof, including pulp and paper. Operators have to exercise 'due diligence' (collect all available information of the timber products that they handle and minimise the risks that these are sourced, processed or traded illegally), keep records of from whom they buy and sell timber and products, and provide assistance to one another in exercising due diligence. However, once an operator deals with FLEGT-licensed timber, 'due diligence' is assured. European Union member states themselves must monitor whether operators follow the EUTR requirements and implement sanctions for non-compliance (Derous and Verhaeghe, 2019; Leipold et al., 2016).

Why does a system like FLEGT exist? The background is of course illegal logging, the harvesting of wood which is not in accordance with national forest laws. Scholars estimate that 15–30 per cent of the world's timber is illegally harvested and traded, and that these figures may rise to 70–90 per cent in individual countries, particularly in tropical timber exporting countries

(Goncalves et al., 2012; Hansen and Treue, 2008; Kleinschmit et al., 2016). Therefore FLEGT is meant to combat these practices. In total, it covers fifteen VPA-countries, as previously stated, and through these countries, it potentially reaches about 420 million ha of forests, so about 10 per cent of the world's forests, where illegal logging might be banned over time (FAO, 2020). But FLEGT is not the only initiative. It started with the G8 'Bali Action Plan' in 2001, committing the G8 countries to promote the rule of law in the forest sector (Nathan et al., 2014). This initiative subsequently led to a partnership between the World Bank, UK, USA and ASEAN, which launched the first regional FLEG (without a 'T') process in Asia and the Pacific. Other regions soon followed, like Africa, South America and Europe. The EU, however, expanded the concept to include the 'T' of trade as a basis for their VPAs.

While the EU adopted its EUTR, the USA introduced its Legal Timber Protection Act (LTPA) and Australia its Illegal Logging Prohibition Act (ILPA) (Leipold et al., 2016). All three aim to ban illegal timber and products thereof from their markets, and all three enforce due diligence or due care upon operators in their timber markets. Together, they create an emerging, yet fragmented, international regime on forest legality based on national law, voluntary international cooperation and market-based licencing schemes (Overdevest and Zeitlin, 2014). However, unlike the EU, the USA and Australia did not parallel their national laws with VPA-like arrangements with timber-exporting countries, although these acts do indeed follow from their regional FLEG processes in the Americas and Oceania, respectively.

If implemented effectively, FLEGT would contribute to achieving (parts of) the Global Forest Goals. For example, GFG 5 on governance frameworks to implement SFM refers to the FLEG processes and calls for a significant reduction of illegal logging and associated trade worldwide (ECOSOC, 2017). With that, FLEGT should also contribute to reversing the loss of forest cover in areas where logging is not legally allowed (GFG 1). Ideally it would also enhance cooperation, coordination and coherence between the EU and tropical timber exporting countries (GFG 6). Potentially, the reach of the FLEGT programme is impressive, about 420 million ha of forests, as previously stated. However, although the programme started nearly fifteen years ago, it is too early to assess whether it already contributes to significantly reducing illegal logging and trade. To reiterate, only one country has recently been able to start exporting FLEGT-licenced wood to the EU (Indonesia).

From my own and colleagues' research, in this case on Ghana, we have seen that the implementation of all the FLEGT requirements has been a very complicated matter at the domestic level of individual countries (Arts and Wiersum, 2010; Beeko and Arts, 2010; Heukels, 2018). Ghana's VPA was signed and entered into force in 2009, more than ten years ago, but FLEGT-licenced timber has not yet arrived in the EU (except for a trial shipment to Rotterdam recently). Reasons are manifold: the technical design of the Wood Tracking System (WTS) as part of the LAS took many more years than anticipated. Several challenges and hiccups had to be overcome, such as digitalisation, the coverage of the entire value chain and the tagging of stumps and logs that is effective and traceable. Slowly but surely, the WTS has nonetheless started to work and the first field audits have been conducted to monitor its performance. Alongside technical challenges, the LAS has also encountered many social-economic ones. Of concern has been the implications of the VPA for smallholders and local communities, whose customary small-scale forestry practices are often 'illegal' according to modern law. Strict enforcement would rather easily criminalise those people who are already living in the poorest conditions. Also, stakeholder participation has been abundant during the design of the Ghanaian VPA, but has reduced during its implementation phase.

4.6 The Hydra of Critical Political Economy

Philosophical pragmatism urges one to organise one's own criticism, as explained in Section 3. An appropriate theoretical counterpoint of the discursive-institutional analysis of co-governance outlined above is *Critical Political Economy* (CPE) (Newell, 2008). Like co-governance theories, it analyses relationships between public and private actors, particularly the state and the market, but contrary to the former, CPE problematises this relationship instead of seeing opportunities for addressing public affairs, including forests (Hansen, 2010; Humphreys, 2006; Park et al., 2008). The key argument is that these public-private arrangements are controlled by economic growth-dependent states and profit-seeking multinationals that have an interest in maintaining the status quo, whereas the true needs of civil society, local communities, indigenous people, forests and nature are ignored or 'co-opted'. Hence, these co-governance initiatives do not sincerely address the *root causes* of deforestation, forest degradation and illegal logging, which is the expansionist capitalist political economy. Therefore, CPE questions the possibility of transforming societies towards justice and sustainability through reformist co-governance arrangements, all the more so since their market-based instruments strengthen capitalism instead of combatting it, leading to 'greenwashing' at best.

This situation is also confirmed by statistics, according to the critics: forest decline just continues (FAO, 2020; Pearce, 2018). Particularly in the remote tropical forest areas of the world, such as the Congo Basin, Kalimantan and Amazonas, the devastating effects of this political economy of deforestation, forest degradation and illegal logging can still be observed, where private and state interests join forces to cash in on forest resources and from land grabbing in unsustainable and often violent ways. The many governance attempts to decapitate this Hydra have obviously not been successful.

Similar criticisms have been voiced, particularly against FLEGT (Derous and Verhaeghe, 2019; Hansen et al., 2018; Rutt et al., 2018). Critics argue, first of all, that its legalistic and technocratic approach denies the *politics* of forest legality, in that social conflicts and social injustices implied in forest laws and practices are not truly addressed. Consequently, FLEGT/VPA holds the danger of reproducing unequal social structures in forestry. Secondly, the question is whether market failures, such as the continuation of illegal logging, can be mitigated by market-based instruments, such as legality licencing. This sounds like a tautology. Finally, ensuring legality is not the same as ensuring sustainability. Legally sourced timber can still be very unsustainable from an ecological or social perspective, if the forest laws concerned still prioritise classical forestry and forest economics over fair and sustainable forest management and conservation.

In addition to the above criticisms, others have argued that the era of – and hope for – effective global governance has also evaporated (Gordon, 2017; Ikenberry, 2011). Currently, in 2021, multilateralism is *under siege* by several political-economic events and trends, for example the resurrection of 'old-fashioned' geopolitics and nationalism by populist leaders, like Putin, Bolsenaro, Erdogan and Trump; the waning power of the United Nations system, not least of the Security Council and the World Trade Organisation; and the slow progress of global environmental governance, particularly international climate change policy. The international regime on illegal logging also expresses these trends and events. What we observe is *not* global governance, but a fragmented regime, based upon regional approaches (USA, Australia, EU; Leipold et al., 2016).

5 Governance Shifts

Whereas Section 4 focused on discourses and arrangements of governance *by* or *with* the state, this section will address governance *without* the state. Of course, one cannot 'think away' or 'bracket' the state as a political entity; it is simply there and even very relevant for strong forms of private self-governance, for example to provide for legal space, tax exemptions or financial incentives to 'nudge' companies towards self-regulation. This is not denied by the so-called new governance scholars, but they do believe that we have entered a new era of governance, with governance of a different *kind*, not just a different *degree* (Pierre and Peters, 2000).

This distinction between 'kind' and 'degree' is however a matter of (inter) subjective interpretation, or even just taste; whether the new governance is considered a 'transformational continuation' of the past or a 'radical breakage' with the past. One can probably argue both ways. This is reinforced by the fact that the 'radical breakage discourse' was particularly strong in the 1990s, after the demise of the Soviet Union and the rise of the New World Order. Accounts of state failure on the one hand and of new governance modes on the other were abundant at that time (Pierre, 2000; Pierre and Peters, 2000). These were nonetheless put into perspective after 9/11 and its aftermath in the 2000s and with the resurgence of nationalism and geopolitics in the 2010s. Most – if not all – governance scholars today will therefore agree that we observe a *transformation* of the state and of the governance landscape rather than a revolutionary change (Arts et al., 2009). Nonetheless, it remains interesting and relevant to address modes of governance without the state, or with the state at a (very far) distance.

5.1 The Chloris of 'Governance without Government'

In much literature, the concept of governance particularly refers to *new* modes of governing that go *beyond* the confines of the state (Rhodes, 1996). Examples are private networks and regimes, self-governance by businesses, private-civic partnerships, markets for ecosystem services and certification programmes (Agrawal et al., 2008; Kickert et al., 1997; Kolk, 2000). Some authors refer to this development as a 'shift from government to governance' (Van Kersbergen and Van Waarden, 2004), others as 'governance without government' (Rosenau and Czempiel, 1992). Much of the 'shift literature' is based on an (implicit) assumption about a diminishing state, which is for example labelled as 'the retreat of the state', 'the hollowing out of the state' or simply 'state decline' in the literature (Pierre, 2000; Strange, 1996). Although Pierre and Peters (2000) still adhere to a state-centric view on governance, and prefer to talk about 'state transformation' rather than 'state decline', they nonetheless unmask the various developments behind this shift. They distinguish three types of 'displacement of state power' in the new governance era: *upward* to international organisations (globalisation), *downward* to subnational authorities (decentralisation) and *outward* to semi-public bodies, civic organisations and private markets (societalisation and privatisation) (see Figure 4).

The first *upward* movement concerns the enormous increase of intergovernmental and non-governmental organisations, international agreements and

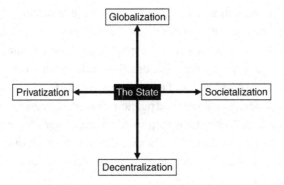

Figure 4 Displacement of state power

international regimes since World War II. At the end of the 2010s, the world held as many as 55,000 international NGOs and 7,500 international organisations, whereas, in 1945, these counts were below 1,000 and 100, respectively (Marshall and Cole, 2011). Also, the number of international agreements adopted – both for trade and environment – grew enormously in the post–World War II era. In the same period, the European Union changed from an intergovernmental organisation, ruled by sovereign nation states, into a supranational body, including a commission, a parliament and a court, that now shares legislative, executive and judicial powers with the member states (Knill and Liefferink, 2013). Of course, such relocation of authority and sovereignty is resisted, today even more than in recent decades. At the same time, this development seems irreversible, since many current problems are transboundary in nature and require international responses, while economies, capital and markets are strongly globalised (Castells, 2000; Waters, 1995).

The second relocation is moving state power *downward* to subnational authorities, be it states (in federal systems) or regions, provinces and cities (in nation-state systems). Such relocation is also referred to as decentralisation and may include de-concentration (redistribution of administrative tasks, without a relocation of authority) or delegation (ibidem, now with a relocation of it) (Work, 2002). Moreover, decentralisation may be political or fiscal in nature, besides being administrative. Reasons to move politics down can be very different: to enhance democracy, by bringing politics closer to the citizens, to increase cost-effectiveness, by reducing the scale of policy-making and problem-solving, or to respond to cultural or ethnic demands for regional or territorial autonomy (Pierre and Peters, 2000). Motives may be more egoistic too, for example when a national government decides to decentralise its unsolved problems and budget cuts to subnational authorities.

Finally, the third, *outward* movement concerns the relocation of state power to societal and private entities (Pierre and Peters, 2000). Examples are NGOs that deliver public services (e.g. in development cooperation), the privatisation of state firms and of public organisations (like state forest enterprises or state forest services), the outsourcing of administrative tasks (e.g. a consultancy that organises public health facilities) and public-private partnerships (like a PPP for building highways). Motivations to privatise state power may partly overlap with those of 'moving it down': to enhance democracy and cost-effectiveness, to cut public budgets and pool resources, or non-state actors take the initiative to organise self-governance.

5.2 Case III: Forest Certification[11]

Still today, much timber that is traded internationally originates from unsustainable sources (IDH, 2020). Several attempts have been made both in the UN and in the International Tropical Timber Organization (ITTO) to negotiate an international agreement – a legally binding treaty or an obligatory certification system – to halt these practices since the early 1980s (Humphreys, 2006). However, all failed due to clashes of interests among importing and exporting countries, rich and poor countries and forestry and conservation advocates (Humphreys, 1996; Kolk, 1996). Given these regulatory failures, several environmental organisations had expressed their wish to do business with industry on sustainable forestry themselves. For example, the World Wildlife Fund (WWF) started a dialogue with industry under the slogan 'Forests are your business' in the UK in 1991 (Bendel, 2000). At that time, on a global level, an NGO-industry led governance initiative on forests had also become expedient, due to political opportunities – intergovernmental failure and presence of strong global NGOs – and timber market structures – strong concentration of business power (Auld, 2014). In 1993, 150 organisations from the business sector, the environmental sector and the human rights movement founded the Forest Stewardship Council (FSC) in Toronto (Cashore et al., 2004; Pattberg, 2007). Today, its headquarters are in Bonn, Germany. The FSC is consequently an interesting example of a *civic-private partnership* to self-regulate sustainable forest management and timber trade.

The overall aim of the FSC is to stop large-scale deforestation, forest degradation, unsustainable forestry and illegal logging around the world by certifying those management and trading practices which enhance the conservation and responsible use of forests. The FSC promotes sustainable forestry and legal trade through the market mechanism. As a consequence, producers

---

[11] This subsection includes text fragments from earlier work, particularly Arts (2002).

and consumers can make a distinction between 'good wood' (FSC-labelled) and 'bad wood' (non-certified) in the marketplace. Therefore, Cashore (2002) labels the FSC forest certification programme as a 'non-state market-driven governance system' (NSMD). This system is based on ten principles, from responsible forest management to respecting community, land property and labour rights, to principles on sustainability, ecology and biodiversity (www.fsc.org), although the claim that certification is able to halt deforestation and forest degradation, is fundamentally challenged by critics. This is because a market-driven governance system focuses primarily on reward, expansion and growth, and not on sustainability, biodiversity conservation and human rights per se (Greenpeace International, 2021). For the latter to occur, the world needs strong policies and regulations, not market instruments.

The FSC principles are elaborated to more practical guidelines, criteria and indicators for forest management planning via either one of two routes, the national or the global (Cashore et al., 2004). Either national sustainable forestry standards can be developed, which at a later stage can then apply for FSC accreditation, or the global FSC principles and guidelines are directly used as a starting point to formulate standards adapted to national circumstances. Until recently, the FSC operated as an accreditation organisation for certification bodies who control the application of the standards (but now a separate organisation does the accreditation, while the FSC is the supreme governing body of the system). This means that certification, monitoring and verification are undertaken by independent, third-party certification and auditor organisations, such as KPMG in Canada, SKAL in the Netherlands, or Smart Wood in the USA.

The FSC initiative has shown rapid growth in coverage since its inception (https://fsc.org/en/page/facts-figures). It started in Mexico in 1991, where a forest area of nearly 90.000 ha was certified. Today, more than 220 million ha of forests in 90 countries – about 5 per cent of the world's forests – are certified by the FSC, although it should be acknowledged that only about 30 million ha of those are to be found in the Global South (Southern America, Africa and Asia). Besides area, the number of so-called Chain-of-Custody (CoC) certifications has also steadily grown over time. These should assure that products that carry the FSC label can be traced back to sustainably managed forests throughout the value chain and can be set aside from other, non-certified products. Today, more than 40,000 organisations, traders and companies worldwide have been granted such a CoC certificate and so are capable of segregating certified and non-certified wood in their business practices. Finally, besides forest area- and CoC-certifications, the FSC system also includes the so-called mixed label. This label allows for up to 30 per cent of 'controlled wood' to be mixed with FSC-certified material. This is an option for businesses who cannot obtain sufficient FSC-certified materials for their produce. Controlled wood nonetheless excludes materials from illegal, protected and genetically modified sources and from practices based on violation of human rights.

The FSC system is voluntary, so forest owners and wood processors are not obliged to become certified. Nonetheless, market pressures (e.g. consumers' demand, competitors that already carry the label) or incentives from governments (e.g. recognition of the system by public authorities) might make the system 'semi-obligatory'. Being certified implies that a forest owner or company lives up to FSC standards, principles, indicators and criteria, for example on labour conditions, forest reserves for biodiversity conservation, sustainable harvest, soil conservation, etc. Once granted, an owner or company will be audited regularly by an independent third party to monitor and verify whether the certificate can be maintained, and which improvements should be made. Being certified is thus rather costly and time-consuming, and should be earned back by a price premium, or by expanding one's market share.

Since the FSC was an NGO-initiated programme, with rather stringent requirements on sustainability, other initiatives soon followed, the Pan-European Forest Certification (PEFC) being the largest today. In 1999, PEFC was launched by European stakeholders, particularly forest owners, as a business alternative to FSC to enhance forest certification more from an economic and trade perspective (Ilie et al., 2018). Pan-European Forest Certification PEFC began as an umbrella organisation to endorse various national forest certification standards in Europe at that time, but today it has a global reach. It includes national schemes such as the Sustainable Forestry Initiative (SFI, USA) and the Canadian Sustainable Forest Management Standard (CSA-FSM, Canada). While the PEFC requirements are 'softer' than those of FSC, the set-up of the systems is rather similar (standardisation, certification, third-party monitoring, etc.). Moreover, the systems have to some extent converged over time; FSC has become more plantation- and industry-friendly, whereas PEFC has tightened requirements on sustainability and monitoring (Cashore et al., 2004). In 2020, FSC and PEFC combined covered about 460 million ha – approximately 11 per cent of the world's forests (although most certified forests are located in the Global North).[12] While these figures are impressive, the question, of course, is whether these certification systems do make a difference on the ground. In other words: do they perform? Until recently, this was simply unknown. For example, Visseren-Hamakers and

---

[12] PEFC covers about 330 million ha (www.pefc.org), FSC about 224 million ha (www.fsc.org/en/facts-figures), but double certification amounts to 95 million ha (www.pefc.org/news/double-certification-fsc-and-pefc-2020-estimation).

Pattberg (2013) and Van der Ven and Cashore (2018) stated a few years back that they could not conclude on FSC's impact due to a lack of (rigorous) field studies.

More recently, Di Girolami (2019) assessed the environmental impact of forest certifications around the world, both FSC and PEFC, through a systematic literature review (SLR).[13] Her review assessed 883 possible titles as a starting point, but only included 29 true impact studies, which cover 49 assessments on flora, fauna and ecosystem services, representing about 13 million ha – or 2.8 per cent – of certified forests around the world. Indicators for environmental impact in these studies relate to floristic composition, tree species diversity, wildlife species, biomass, dead wood, forest disturbance, carbon stock, forest areas for conservation and reduced deforestation among others. Now thirty-two of these forty-nine environmental impact assessments report positive results, fifteen show no impact, while two report a negative one. These figures imply a 'success rate' of about 65 per cent, which seems quite a good performance for forest certification. However, one must be aware of 'positive bias' in such scholarly literature.[14] This bias was tested for in a second step where only assessments from this SLR with the highest quality and rigour scores based on quasi-experimental design, are taken into account. At this point the figure drops to 50 per cent (five out of ten). Consequently, I conclude from this SLR that about half of environmental impact assessments on forest certification report robust positive results. However, one should be careful in generalising these findings beyond the rather low number of studies covered by this SLR (although still covering 2.8 per cent of certified forests around the world, including areas in the tropics). In addition, the *degree* of positive environmental impact could not be derived from this SLR.

The above results match another SLR on forest certification quite well, although it particularly focuses on the tropics and FSC (see https://news .mongabay.com/2017/09/does-forest-certification-really-work/). It shows that in 70 per cent of the cases (sixty-one of eighty-seven measurements) certified forest management performs better than conventional logging on environmental indicators, but this figure drops to 50 per cent if only studies with 'stronger evidence' are included (ten out of twenty). Besides, this SLR also covers the

---

[13] This systematic literature review was published as an MSc thesis; I supervised the study and it was reviewed by an independent academic expert on SLR. In addition, I also checked the impact assessments and quality and rigor scores of a sample of studies (N=10) in order to guarantee intersubjective reliability. The calculations in this text are my own, not Di Girolami's.

[14] For example, *researcher* bias (researchers have a positive attitude towards certification and favour positive conclusions, either consciously or unconsciously); *methodological* bias (methods are not sufficiently rigorous to determine co-variation, let alone causality); and *publication* bias (scientific journals prefer to publish positive results).

social-economic impacts of forest certification. For social impact, positive effects were observed in 62 per cent and 71 per cent of measurements ('all evidence' N=29 and 'stronger evidence' N=7, respectively); for economic impact, this figure amounts to 46 per cent (only 'weaker evidence' available; N=80).

Although neither implemented to its full potential nor successful everywhere, the forest certification programmes do indeed contribute to achieving (part of) the Global Forest Goals, given the performances previously reported, particularly GFG 1 and 2. Through promoting SFM, forest certification contributes to reversing the loss of forest cover in various locations, while it also enhances environmental, social and economic benefits from forests in many instances, although negative impacts are also reported by a minority of studies.

5.3 Experimentalist Governance

A relatively new concept that also matches the 'shifts idea' rather well is 'experimentalist governance'. Its theorists observe the emergence of 'transnational new governance' (TNG) *besides* 'international old governance' (IOG) (Overdest and Zeitling, 2014; Sabel and Zeitling, 2012). Although this is interpreted as a shift towards new modes of governance here, theorists would never claim that the latter has completely replaced the former; they *both* exist. In this respect, the theorists differ from the 'shift scholars' of the 1990s, who at that time strongly believed in 'state decline' (see Subsection 5.1). Table 3 summarises the differences. International old governance largely equates classical regime building (Keohane, 1984; Rittberger, 1993). States acknowledge the need for international regulation of a transboundary problem that (potentially) affect their security, environmental and/or economic interests; hence, their national interests converge, so they decide to build an 'international regime', a set of principles, norms, rules and procedures to regulate the problem concerned. Ideally, such a regime consists of a hard core, a legally binding treaty, and a number of other legal instruments besides it, to enforce targets, timetables and implementation measures upon the participating countries. In case of noncompliance, the regime is ideally able to impose sanctions upon countries concerned. This is possible particularly when a 'benign' hegemon acts as a governor of the international regime and pushes through compliance and sanctioning.

The past has shown that such IOG regimes are hard to ever agree upon. The climate regime is a good illustration (Gupta and Van Asselt, 2017; Rabe, 2007). The Kyoto Protocol of 1997 *does* include binding targets and timetables to reduce the emission of greenhouse gases by developed countries, but these are

Table 3 International old oovernance (IOG) versus transnational new governance (TNG)

International old governance (IOG)	Transnational new governance (TNG)
International regime based on either convergence of state interests or on hegemonic power	Fragmented regime complex; multiple actors, multiple levels, multiple sectors; uncertainty and goal-seeking
1 Targets and timetables	1 Framework goals
2 Top-down implementation	2 National discretion
3 Sanctioning of non-compliance	3 Peer review
4 Stick to the given rules	4 Regular revision
5 Institutionalisation	5 Experimenting, learning-by-doing

far from strict (-5 per cent in 2008–12 compared to 1990). While the negotiations started with much more ambitious targets (-20 per cent in 2010 compared to 1990), these were considerably loosened during the negotiation process, because countries knew these would become binding. Therefore, the current Paris Agreement (2015) does *not* include binding targets and timetables for individual countries, but one overall long-term collective goal (to hold the increase of global average temperature to well below 2 °C above pre-industrial levels, and preferably below 1.5 °C). Within that framework goal, countries can design their own Nationally Determined Contribution (NDC) to achieving it, and every five years the international community will check whether countries are individually and collectively on the right track. If not, they will be pushed by the international community (while probably being blamed and shamed by NGOs) to strengthen their policies. Actually, with this new approach, the climate regime has entered the sphere of experimentalist governance. Framework goals are set at the global level, national implementation is left to the discretion of individual countries, their performances are regularly peer reviewed by the international community and national policies will be revised, if necessary.

The above explanation assumes that countries move from IOG to TNG because the latter serves their interests better (read: it is easier for them to circumvent ambitious international goals and targets through national policy measures that are less strict). This may be part of the story, but another part is the nature of the policy issues at hand (Sabel and Zeitling, 2012). When the issues are: (1) complex and volatile, (2) hold epistemic uncertainties, (3) include many players at different administrative levels, (4) are characterised by goal-seeking instead of goal-attainment, (5) raise many value conflicts and (6) lack a benign hegemon that is able and willing to push through a collective policy, a TNG approach matches the situation much better than an IOG approach. However, TNG regimes may differ in origin, shape and design process. Overdest and Zeitling (2014) distinguish four pathways of increasing experimentalism and learning in forest governance: (1) the emergence of a private experimentalist regime as a response to government failure (like the forest certification initiatives as a response to the failure of an international legally binding forest convention); (2) the emergence of a (loose) system of international benchmarking (like the partial convergence of those forest certification initiatives through mutual benchmarking); (3) the emergence of a regime complex that (loosely) coordinates national and/or regional initiatives (like the current international forest arrangement that connects SFM initiatives worldwide); and (4) the emergence of an unilateral trade regime by a state or a group of states as a response to a lack of multilateral coverage (like the FLEGT initiative by the EU).

5.4 Case IV: REDD+[15]

A relatively new governance arrangement is *Payment for Ecosystem Services*, or PES (Costanza et al., 1997; Farber et al., 2002). The core idea is to pay landowners for services that were once provided for free, such as water regulation, soil protection and climate change regulation through land use, management and conservation. Without such payments, these services cannot compete with monetary values in the marketplace. For example, if a forest owner can choose between forest utilisation (timber) or forest conservation (water and erosion regulation), he/she will choose for the former in case cash is needed. This may occur at the cost of environmental services, the so-called external effects. Now with PES in place, this situation might be reversed if prices are indeed competitive. An owner may then choose to prioritise conservation over utilisation or integrate both. Crucial for such PES markets is that interested buyers are in place. Such may be the case if, for example, consumers need clean water or protection from landslides, or if policies oblige producers to compensate for their external effects.

An experiment with PES in forest governance is REDD+ (Levin et al., 2008). This acronym stands for 'Reducing Emissions from Deforestation and forest Degradation', while the '+' signifies the role of forest conservation, sustainable management of forests and enhancement of forest carbon stocks in reducing emissions in developing countries (UNFCCC, 2010). Since deforestation and

---

[15] This subsection includes text fragments from earlier work, particularly Arts and colleagues (2019).

forest degradation are said to contribute to about 12–17 per cent of worldwide greenhouse gas emissions (Bosetti and Lubowski, 2010), avoiding these phenomena helps to mitigate climate change. Now, the main idea of REDD+ is that developing countries are paid for achieving less deforestation, more conservation and better management practices through so-called carbon credits that can be traded on international carbon markets. At the same time, developed countries can buy these credits on those markets which helps them to implement their NDCs under the Paris Agreement. To date, these markets do not function well, and as a result REDD+ is currently predominantly financed through (inter) governmental funds.

First known as 'avoided deforestation' (AD) and discussed as a mitigation option at the United Nations Framework Convention on Climate Change (UNFCCC) in the early 2000s, AD subsequently became RED, REDD and REDD+, with the concept expanding to incorporate forest conservation, management and use (Den Besten et al., 2014). Whereas RED was a proposal tabled by Costa Rica and Papua New Guinea in 2005, known for their interest in forest conservation, REDD also included the interests of countries that particularly suffered from forest degradation, while the '+' in REDD+ satisfied the needs of developing countries that particularly focused on forest use and management. Eligible REDD+ activities were subsequently outlined in the Bali Action Plan resulting from the 13th Conference of Parties to the UNFCCC (COP 13) in 2007. In between, international bodies such as the World Bank, the United Nations Development Programme (UNDP) and the United Nations Environment Programme (UNEP) and developed countries (notably Norway, Australia, the UK, the USA and Germany), started REDD+ programmes and funds, and developing countries entered so-called readiness activities to prepare for participation in REDD+. Currently, REDD+ is being piloted in hundreds of projects around the world through bilateral initiatives (e.g. between Norway and Indonesia) and in multilateral initiatives (through the UN and the World Bank). In the meantime, REDD+ has also become part of Article 5 of the Paris Agreement from 2015, and as such is a legitimate means to implement the Paris commitments.

However, many observers, stakeholders and scholars have been critical about REDD+ (Arts et al., 2019; Fletcher et al., 2016; Phelps et al., 2010). Initial debates focused on offsetting, additionality, permanence, leakage and finance (Buckley et al., 2018). For example, critical NGOs and some developing countries questioned the legitimacy of developed countries offsetting their emissions through REDD+; should the latter not focus on emission *reduction* at home instead of compensation *elsewhere*? In addition, the permanence and additionality of REDD+ initiatives have been discussed. How to make sure that additional carbon sequestration occurs through REDD+ projects, and what baseline should be used to address additionality? How to guarantee that carbon sinks become permanent over time, while under pressure of agricultural expansion, for example? And how to make sure that deforestation practices are not relocated to other forested regions (leakage)? From the start there was also a heated debate on finance. Who should pay for REDD+ and through what mechanism? Since carbon markets were hardly developed at the inception of REDD+ and carbon prices have also remained (far) too low during the last decade to be able to compete with other market values, one can find many sceptics of REDD+ as a true PES mechanism. So far, projects have mainly been financed by governmental funds, mobilised by the UN and World Bank, or by individual donors. Hence, so far REDD+ is no PES at all, but, at best, a FES ('Funds for Ecosystem Services').

More recent debates have focused on the operationalisation and implementation of REDD+, such as result-based payments (RBPs), social and environmental safeguards and co-benefits, and measurement, reporting and verification (MRV) (Angelsen, 2017; Visseren-Hamakers et al., 2012). For example, the Bali Action Plan requires REDD+ projects to measure changes in net carbon emissions resulting from project activities in order to identify real performance. In addition, COP19 adopted the Warsaw Framework for REDD+, which states that results-based payments can only occur once social and environmental safeguards have been addressed. And Measurement, Reporting and Verification (MRV) requirements of RBPs were subsequently elaborated at COP24 in Katowice, Poland, December 2018.

If implemented effectively, REDD+ would contribute to achieving (parts of) the Global Forest Goals, particularly GFG 1, 2, 3 and 4, namely to reverse the loss of forests through SFM (the '+' in REDD+), to enhance the environmental benefits from forests (carbon stocking through REDD+), to increase the area of protected forests (through avoiding deforestation in REDD+ areas) and to mobilise new and additional financial resources (through REDD+ funds and carbon markets). At least two attempts have been made to review the performance of REDD+ so far, as reported in the scholarly literature. Firstly, a group of authors tried to take stock of the impacts of REDD+ in a special issue (Arts et al., 2019). According to them, the initiative definitely exhibits potential. It can contribute to achieving international objectives and targets (besides the Global Forest Goals, the Paris Agreement, the Aichi targets and the SDGs); it may also bring additional income to communities who sustainably manage their forests against the trend of forest conversion; it can reduce deforestation once various approaches are smartly combined (private sector, juridical approach); and it may re-energise 'old-fashioned' forest management approaches (such as community forestry and forest restoration). At the same time, the special issue shows that rhetoric is often stronger than evidence on the ground; that short-term, administrative interests easily overshadow long-term environmental ones; that REDD+ rules may adversely interact with state and customary institutions; and that REDD+ often lacks legitimacy by excluding local people.

The second literature review of REDD+ performance synthesised eight studies (Simonet et al., 2018). It reports that its *reach* is substantial – about 350 initiatives in 53 countries, covering an area of over 43 million ha today – but that its *impact* on forest and carbon is hardly known due to a lack of (rigorous) impact studies. Six of the eight available publications nonetheless report positive impacts, particularly less deforestation than before the REDD + initiative started (N=2; before-after measurement), or compared to non-REDD+ areas (N=4; quasi-experimental). Fewer forest fires and more carbon stocking were also observed, but by single studies.

Without a doubt, REDD+ can be considered an experimentalist governance regime. First of all, it is based on a framework goal, without specific targets and timetables. The idea is to facilitate the conservation and sustainable management of forests in order to reduce greenhouse gas emissions by forests and to increase the sequestration and stocking of these gases. Secondly, it is an international regime, but national governments and stakeholders have lots of discretion to set their own ambition and organise their own approach, although they are of course subject to certain rulebooks and financial requirements once they join REDD+ programmes of the UN, World Bank or of individual countries like Norway. Moreover, they also have to report their performance to these bodies, or to the UNFCCC, in case REDD+ is part of nationally determined contributions (NDCs) of countries to implement the Paris Agreement. Thirdly, REDD+ is strongly characterised by learning-by-doing and by policy learning. One can observe a diversity of initiators, initiatives and approaches. As said, several programmes and funds exist (UN, World Bank, bilateral), participants experiment with voluntary carbon markets and various approaches are tried. For example, Turnhout and colleagues (2017) distinguish three: carbon-centred, co-benefit-centred and landscape-centred REDD+. The first fully focuses on carbon sequestration and carbon stocks, the second on benefits for people and biodiversity, besides carbon performance, and the third on how REDD+ initiatives relate to other land uses in the broader landscape, hoping that drivers of deforestation and forest degradation can be better addressed through this landscape approach.

5.5 The Hydra of Neo-liberalisation

Some critics interpret the (partial) shift from forest government to forest governance as part of the broader neo-liberal agenda (Humphreys, 2006). Neo-liberalism is characterised, amongst others, by privatisation, marketisation, self-regulation and entrepreneurial freedom (Arts et al., 2009; Castree, 2010). Being first implemented as a policy programme by Reagan and Thatcher in the 1980s, it became the dominant, global political-economic ideology of the 1990s and 2000s, although many variations exist in national political economies and in international regimes (Schmidt, 2002). In policy-making, neo-liberalism is expressed with much greater emphasis on market-based instruments (MBIs) for regulating collective goods, like certification and PES, and on self-regulation by companies and communities – phenomena exactly as described in this section, for example forest certification, PES and REDD+. While many governance advocates consider this a positive development, offering new opportunities for more cost-effective governance than classical state regulation, critics of neo-liberalism warn for further expansion and intrusion of capitalist principles (such as self-interest, monetarisation and profit-making), in the governance of collective goods, like forests (Castree, 2010; Fletcher et al., 2016; McAfee, 1999). According to them, 'selling nature to save it' is a devastating route, a Hydra so to speak.

The most oft-heard criticism is that the neo-liberal conservation approach will further commercialise nature and thus potentially intensify the exploitation of natural resources instead of protecting them. While advocates believe that allocating nature a market price makes it more competitively viable, vis-à-vis agriculture and other land use options, and so offers landowners and land managers an incentive to conserve or sustainably use it, the critics pose the counterargument that rich entrepreneurs and capital-intensive investors will always be able and willing to accelerate nature's exploitation against prevailing market prices. Since there is no limit on capitalist growth, there will be no limit on nature's exploitation, whatever price is being asked. As a result, nature will be truly victimised under a neo-liberal regime. Hence, market prices for nature are not justified alternatives for (binding) rules, targets and timetables for conservation.

Similar criticisms are also voiced against forest certification in particular (Greenpeace International, 2021). As certification is a market-driven govern-ance system – or in other terms, a neo-liberal MBI – it is trapped in the logic of economic freedom, reward, growth and expansion. Consequently, it falls short of avoiding deforestation, rejecting plantation expansion, protecting forest biodiversity, respecting all indigenous land rights, and offering full transparency and traceability in value chains. Such criticisms, however, are aimed particularly at PEFC, and less so at FSC. For the critics, certification of forest areas and value chains can never be a credible alternative to strict and binding (inter)governmental policies and regulations on the conservation and sustainable use of forests, and on the rights and needs of forest-dependent people.

6 Governance Norms

Whereas the previous sections focused on the *analytics* of forest governance ('the modes' and 'the shifts'), this section will mainly address *normative* aspects of forest governance ('the norms'). Of course, one cannot easily separate analysis from ethics, or facts from values (see Section 3), but again, it is a matter of *degree* as to where the emphasis is placed. Below, I focus on 'good' forest governance. In so doing, I take Participatory Forest Management (PFM) as a case, since 'participation' is one of the good forest governance principles (FAO-PROFOR, 2011). The FAO introduced PFM in the 1980s to give local communities a voice in decision-making on surrounding forests, and hence a role in local forest management practices (FAO, 2016). Although new at that time, PFM has built on older traditions of indigenous and community forestry (Wiersum, 2009), and matured and expanded into the principles of forest governance that we recognise today.

6.1 'Bad', 'Good' and 'Good Enough' Governance

'Good governance' has become an important discourse in international affairs since the early 1990s, but its meaning is rather fluid, and differs per institution; Gisselquist (2012: 1) offers this description:

> In general, work by the World Bank and other multilateral development banks on good governance addresses economic institutions and public sector management, including transparency and accountability, regulatory reform, and public sector skills and leadership. Other organizations, like the United Nations, European Commission and OECD, are more likely to highlight democratic governance and human rights, aspects of political governance avoided by the Bank.

So, governance is generally considered 'good' if it is characterised by the rule of law, stakeholder participation, democratic and transparent decision-making and accountability of politicians. It is also associated with efficient and effective states and markets, with smart management of natural, human and financial resources, and with fair allocation and equitable sharing of resources and benefits (Bevir, 2012; Kjaer, 2004; Woods, 2000).

Good governance did not just drop out the air. Important (related) drivers for its emergence were the following (Weiss, 2000): (1) inefficient bureaucracies and markets as well as monetary hyperinflation in several developing countries in the 1980s, which led international institutions like the IMF and the World Bank to design 'structural adjustment programmes', including public administration reform, in exchange for financial aid to those countries; (2) the increasing illegitimacy of repressive regimes at that time (e.g. the Khmer in Cambodia, Idi Amin in Uganda and Duvalier in Haiti); (3) the demise of the Soviet bloc in the late 1980s; (4) a new wave of democratisation just after the fall of the Berlin Wall in the early 1990s; and (5) a boom in human rights advocacy by individual countries, the UN and many NGOs in those decades. 'Bad' governance – in terms of unelected and unaccountable governments, endemic corruption and violation of human rights – was deemed less acceptable by the international community. And so 'good governance' emerged as the natural opposite.

Over time, the good governance discourse was complemented with 'good enough governance' and 'better governance' (Grindle, 2007). Reasons were threefold (Weiss, 2000). Firstly, it was impossible for many (developing) countries to live up to all the good governance criteria and indicators; the assignment was simply too complex. Selection and prioritisation were necessary. Secondly, initial pleas for good governance were very much inspired by neo-liberalism – monetarist economics on the one hand and new public management on the other – with (too) much emphasis on the role of the private sector in managing public affairs. Whereas hyperinflation was successfully fought in several countries, the reform of the public sector meant its neglect or even its demolition in several cases, so imbalance between the public and private sectors arose. Thirdly, the strong emphasis on political and human rights was complemented by socio-economic rights, not least through the growing power of China (and others) in the international community. Consequently, democracy is one thing and human development another; in the Global South, perhaps the latter is as or even more important than the former.

6.2 The Chloris of 'Good (Enough) Forest Governance'

In the forest sector, too, good governance has become a very relevant discourse. One of the most well-known frameworks in this field is the one of FAO-PROFOR (2011: 10; see Figure 5). It was designed in a series of expert workshops organised by FAO, World Bank-PROFOR and Chatham House in the period 2009–11, and in which other organisations like ITTO, the World Resources Institute (WRI), EU-FLEGT, UN-REDD and the Swedish International Development Cooperation Agency (SIDA) also participated.

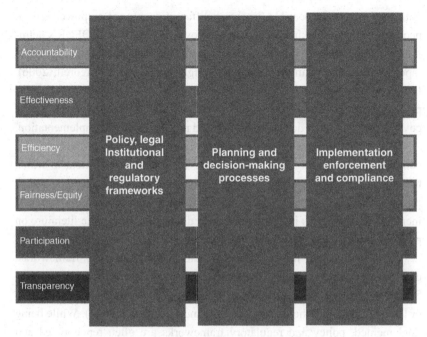

Figure 5 Pillars and principles of good governance (Source: FAO-PROFOR, 2011; reprint permitted)

The aim of the framework is to facilitate countries to diagnose, monitor and improve upon their forest governance performance. It is also meant to foster dialogue among stakeholders in the forest sector and to compare countries' performances. It builds upon established principles for good governance – accountability, effectiveness, efficiency, fairness, equity, participation and transparency – and relevant pillars in the policy cycle – legal frameworks, decision-making processes and implementation trajectories.

It does not make sense to detail all aspects of the framework here, but to zoom in only on those elements that are pertinent to the PFM case study below: *participation* (the key characteristic of PFM) and *implementation* (because we are particularly interested in performance). The FAO-PROFOR framework defines participation as 'involvement of citizens and stakeholders in decision-making, either directly or through legitimate intermediaries representing their interests'. This is a straightforward definition, but one should realise that it is also a rather 'weak' interpretation of participation. If one takes Arnstein's (1969) participation ladder, it is positioned somewhere in the middle, between information and consultation offered by authorities to citizens (the weaker modes of participation) and delegated power and citizen control over public issues (the stronger modes of participation). Hence, participation sounds nice, but many modes are possible, implying different degrees of empowerment of people in decision-making processes. Moreover, given FAO-PROFOR's definition, participation can refer to different forms of democracy, either as *direct* input in decision-making or *indirect* through representation (Teorell, 2006). However, given that governance principles relate to *all* pillars of the policy process in Figure 5, it is surprising that the FAO-PROFOR definition only covers participation in decision-making, and not, for example, implementation.

The third pillar in the figure concerns 'implementation, enforcement and compliance'. According to FAO-PROFOR, it 'examines the extent to which the policy, legal, institutional and regulatory frameworks are implemented; it further considers the level of effectiveness, efficiency and equitability of implementation'. Again, this is a straightforward description, given the literature on policy sciences and policy evaluation (Birkland, 2005; Dunn, 2016). However, it should be said that in particular institutional and regulatory frameworks, effectiveness and equitability will be addressed in the PFM case study in Subsection 6.3.[16] Also, one should be careful in separating the policy phases – or the three pillars of the framework – too much (Sabatier, 2007). While being implemented, policy and regulatory frameworks are often renegotiated and redefined locally, and are hence, in many instances, implemented differently than originally planned (Arts et al., 2014).

Obviously, 'good *enough* forest governance' does not seem to have a strong foothold in the forest governance literature. Just a few references could be found (for example in Springate-Baginski and Wollenberg, 2010; and in Savenije and Van Dijk, 2010). These also express the need to contextualise (Western) good governance principles and criteria to relevant situations in the Global South, and to subject all those good forest governance ambitions to a reality check.

6.3 Case V: Participatory Forest Management[17]

Participatory Forest Management (PFM) has become an influential approach in the management of forests around the world over the last couple of decades, particularly in relation to community forestry and co-management of forests in the Global South (Agrawal, 2001; Arnold, 2001; Wiersum, 2009). Participatory Forest Management is defined by FAO (2016) as 'processes and mechanisms that enable those people who have a direct stake in forest resources to be part of decision making in forest management'. As a response to large-scale state forestry and commercial timber production, that often exclude local people,

---

[16] Hence, legal and economic aspects and efficiency will not be covered in the PFM case, which relates to my background and focus, and to the availability of data.

[17] This Subsection includes text fragments from earlier work, particularly Arts and De Koning (2017).

and building upon both indigenous traditions and modern approaches of forest management, PFM puts the decisional power of local people, the fulfilment of their forest-related livelihoods and sustainable forest management first (Arts and De Koning, 2017). Forests may, may not, or may partially be owned by communities, and their management is often practiced in various degrees of collaboration with state forest agencies, donor organisations, knowledge institutions and/or companies. At one end of the spectrum, forest management is fully community-based, and the forests concerned are 100 per cent owned by the community. Whereas, at the other end, communities just participate in some of the state forest management practices on public lands. Because of this variation, several terminologies are used to refer to these practices (community forestry, community-based forest management, community-managed forests, collaborative forest management, participatory forest management, joint forest management and forest co-management). I prefer the term PFM here, because it is often used in the scholarly literature and in management practices, and the 'Participatory' of PFM directly relates to one of the good forest governance principles.

The central idea behind PFM is that local (co)management of forests, which is decided upon either by communities alone or in conjunction with forest departments, is more effective than management led by central state institutions. This is because 'sense ownership', either legal or practical, and hence responsibility, is given back to the people (Charnley and Poe, 2007). Early in the 1970s, the idea of community participation, both for better forest management and for improving people's livelihoods, was already practiced in a few countries. Scientists and NGOs advocated the approach and it was intensively discussed in the FAO at a global level (Arnold, 2001; FAO, 1978; Umans, 1993). Later, these ideas entered as norms into international law, both as hard and soft law, for example in Agenda 21, the Rio Forest Principles, the Convention on Biological Diversity and the Non-Legally Binding Instrument on All Types of Forests (Arts and Babili, 2013). Such ideas and norms have in turn travelled to national levels, where they became embedded in forest law and policy, or strengthened already existing local PFM practices in countries. For example, India, Nepal, Mexico, Bolivia, Kenya and Tanzania have pioneered different forms of PFM from the early 1990s onwards, and many countries, from Ethiopia to Albania, followed later (Baynes et al., 2015; Charnley and Poe, 2007).

The basis of PFM is found in critiques of 'state forestry' and 'coercive conservation' (Agrawal, 2001; Dressler et al., 2010). Traditionally, the political response to forest loss has been the nationalisation of forest areas and top-down, state-led forest management and conservation approaches, on the premise that local people are caught in a 'tragedy of the commons' (Hardin, 1968). This tragedy fosters overuse of the resource through growing populations, increasing demands and lack of knowledge to rationally manage and conserve resources (Scott, 1998). However, 'state forestry' hardly delivered on its promises, particularly in the tropics, where state intervention was often weak, incompetent and/or corrupt (Agrawal, 2001). Moreover, 'coercive conservation', which was based on the classical Western Yellowstone model of national parks and protected areas, led to the exclusion of people from their lands and violation of their forest rights in many tropical countries, thus fuelling debates on 'doing conservation otherwise' (Dressler et al., 2010). Consequently, discourses on proper forest management and conservation drastically shifted over time (Umans, 1993; Wiersum, 2009).

The global debate on community-based natural resource management (CBNRM) has been very influential. Various scholars have argued that the 'tragedy of the commons' thesis is theoretically flawed. They have also empirically falsified it by showing many examples of successful customary management systems of scarce resources from all over the world (Agrawal, 2001; Ostrom, 1990). This scholarly literature had an enormous impact on global debates on natural resource management, such as in the FAO, World Bank, UNEP, UNDP and more recently, the UNFF. Increasingly, international policy makers, diplomats and NGOs began to advocate the CBNRM approach and, as already said, references to it emerged in all kinds of policy documents. At the same time, local communities and indigenous peoples increasingly propagated and strengthened their (forest) rights in international fora, fuelling the CBNRM debate from within and across their transnational networks (Dupuits and Ongolo, 2020). Subsequently, this 'glocal' discourse slowly but surely entered national policies and local practices.

The history of PFM exhibits various phases in which different approaches were experimented with. Wiersum (2009) distinguishes the following: (1) a *conservation* phase, in which PFM mainly targeted the conservation and rehabilitation of community forests; (2) a *collaborative* phase, in which cooperation and joint decision-making of state agencies, donors, local communities and indigenous people were put centre stage in order to alleviate poverty and sustainably manage forests; (3) an *empowerment* phase, in which the democratic and forest rights of local communities and indigenous people were emphasised, building upon the UN Declaration on the Rights of Indigenous People (UNDRIP) and the FPIC principle (the right to free, prior and informed consent) included in it; and (4) an *entrepreneurial* phase, in which PFM initiatives have been related to the establishment of local enterprises and to global value chains, including the initiation of community-based forest certification, to serve niche markets for certified tropical timber in the Global North (Molnar, 2004; Wiersum et al., 2011). Of course, these phases did not neatly follow consecutively; rather, they have been overlapping and many aspects of these do still exist in parallel today.

In all its diversity, PFM now covers about 600 million ha around the world (RRI, 2014).[18] An impressive figure indeed, but the question is of course whether it makes a difference on the ground, and – from the perspective of this Element – contributes to achieving the UN's Global Forest Goals. Over the years, a vast body of scholarly literature on the performance of PFM has emerged. The current consensus is that – overall – the results of PFM are *mixed* (Arts and De Koning, 2017; Baynes et al., 2015; Charnley and Poe, 2007). Many programmes and projects are rather successful, but others have failed too. Moreover, forests have generally benefitted more from PFM than people (Bowler et al., 2012). And for as far as the latter have done so, the relatively well-off gained more from these programmes and projects than the poor, which is often referred to as 'elite capture'.

In 2019, Di Girolami assessed the environmental impact of PFM in more detail (in addition to the impacts of forest certification; see Subsection 5.2).[19] Di Girolami's literature review assessed 2,082 potential titles as a starting point, but only included thirty-six true impact studies, and through these, eighty-nine assessments on flora, fauna and ecosystem services, representing nearly 6 million ha – or about 1 per cent – of PFM forests around the world. Indicators for environmental impact in these studies refer to basal area, canopy cover, deforestation, forest biodiversity, forest degradation, forest growth, forest regeneration, wildlife, biomass, carbon stock and others, for example. Seventy-two of those assessments report positive environmental impacts on one or more of these indicators, fourteen show no impact, whereas three assessments report a negative impact. These figures imply a 'success rate' of ~81 per cent (seventy-two out of eighty-nine), which seems quite a high performance for PFM. Like in the case of certification, one can test for 'positive

---

[18] The most robust figure on the size of PFM (both community forestry by indigenous peoples and local communities, and co-management of forests by them and governmental authorities) is RRI's one: 511 million ha in 2013 (RRI, 2014). This area increased from 383 million ha in 2002. However, the report also claims that growth in area *owned* by indigenous peoples and local communities slowed down to 20 per cent in the period 2008–13 as compared to 2002–7 (be aware, this figure is *not* about co-management). Therefore, it is assumed that – based on extrapolation from the 2008–13 period – the annual increase in area is about 5 million ha in the period 2014–20. The 2020 estimation then amounts to about 546 million ha. However, RRI's study represents 90 per cent of the world's forests, so a correction would imply an estimation of the global surface of PFM of about 600 million ha in 2020.

[19] Di Girolami refers to PFM as CFM, or community-based forest management. I stick to PFM in the following.

bias' by only taking those assessments from this SLR into account with the highest quality and rigour scores. On doing so, the 'success rate' drops a bit (72 per cent; thirteen out of eighteen assessments). Consequently, it can be concluded from this SLR that about three-quarters of environmental impact assessments on PFM report robust positive results. However, one should be careful in generalising these findings beyond the studies and forest areas covered in this SLR. In addition, the *degree* of positive environmental impact could not be derived from this SLR.

The above results, to a certain extent, match another SLR on PFM (see https://news.mongabay.com/2017/09/does-community-based-forest-manage ment-work-in-the-tropics). It shows that in 55 per cent of the cases (thirty-eight of sixty-nine measurements) PFM performs better than 'no-PFM-situations' in relation to impact on environmental indicators, but this figure drops to 47 per cent if only studies with 'stronger evidence' are included (fourteen out of thirty). In addition, this SLR also covers the social-economic impacts of PFM. For social impact, positive effects were observed in 45 per cent and 37 per cent of measurements ('all evidence' N=78 and 'stronger evidence' N=19, respectively); for economic impact, this figure amounts to 50 per cent (mainly 'weaker evidence' available; N=36).

Despite being neither implemented to its full potential nor being successful everywhere, PFM does contribute to achieving (parts of) the Global Forest Goals, given the results of the SLRs previously highlighted, particularly GFG 1, 2, 5 and 6. Through promoting SFM at local levels, it reverses the loss of forest cover and quality in many localities, while also enhancing the livelihoods of forest-dependent people in multiple situations. Moreover, PFM engages local communities and indigenous people in forest management and so enhances cooperation between them and forest officials. Yet, it is striking that the environmental performance of PFM is much better than the social-economic one, with negative impacts on local communities also being reported in various studies. Hence, under this governance arrangement, forests seem better off than people.

6.4 The Hydra of Governmentality

The Subsection 6.3 showed that PFM produces mixed results and does fall short in the social-economic realm. Yet, many scholars believe that performances can be improved once success and failure factors – such as key institutional, social, political and silvicultural components of PFM – are better addressed by pol- icies, programmes and projects (Agrawal, 2001; Arts and De Koning, 2017; FAO, 2016). Such optimism is not shared by all, because the 'participatory approach' in development has been fundamentally criticised. The best example is probably the book *Participation: The New Tyranny?* (Cooke and Kothari, 2001). The authors argue that participatory approaches have often resulted in their opposite, namely 'an illegitimate and unjustified exercise of power' (which is one dictionary definition of 'tyranny'). The participatory approach sounds nice – bottom-up development that is community- and people-centred – but, according to the critics, the underlying discourses and emerging practices serve the interests of the donor industry and the most powerful community members best. The main reason as to why it works like this is that participatory development advocates an individualist, Western, technocratic and procedural approach, while power relations are not addressed. Consequently, unequal social structures and hierarchical cultures are perpetuated, if not reinforced, by participatory approaches, and marginalised people are not or barely empowered. The authors of the book therefore do not believe that improving approaches to address success/failure factors, as identified previously, will lead to better outcomes. In contrast, they advocate a 'radical reflexivity' on Western development discourses, on recognising local realities, and on addressing internal and external power circuits in development practices.

Several contributors to *Participation: The New Tyranny?* apply a Foucauldian approach. In so doing, they use the notion of 'thick' discourse (see Section 3) to show that the participatory approach is biased towards Western conceptualisations of human nature, of development and of democracy, thus excluding local realities and cultures, and reproducing power structures and social hierarchies. Although Foucault does not exactly specify how a discourse should be defined (see Foucault, 1971), he refers to it as an ensemble of discursive events, of language in practice – classifications, taboos, truths, disciplines, etc. – that produces the generally accepted subjects and objects of a society (the 'normal'), consequently excluding others (the 'abnormal'). As a result, discourse is strongly associated with terms like normalisation, disciplining, power and exclusion. With that, it goes beyond the realm of language as such, and includes social practices and materialities too.

Foucault (2002) also studied the role of discourse in government and governance, which is highly relevant for this Element. He refers to it as 'governmentality', also interpreted as 'the reason of state' or 'the art of governing' (Bose et al., 2012; Dean, 2010). In order to survive over time, serve its own interests and act on behalf of the collective, it is crucial for a government to keep control of society, but the technologies to realise this have dramatically changed. Fletcher (2010), building upon Foucault's work, distinguishes four governmentalities: 'truth governmentality' by religious empires (ruling through God's laws), 'sovereignty governmentality' by traditional kings (ruling through kinship and blunt force), 'disciplinary governmentality' by the modern state (ruling through values, norms, and rules, and so disciplining people into obedient citizens) and 'neo-liberal governmentality' by the late-modern state (ruling people through economic incentive structures). In all these governmentalities, discourses are crucial governing techniques to shape the political and social legitimacies of the statehood concerned, like hegemonic discourses on God, the monarchy, the rule of law or economic growth. Now, PFM can probably be considered as being part of the latter two. Fletcher writes (2010: 177): 'Community-based conservation might be seen to embody alternate strands of disciplinarity and neo-liberalism, depending upon whether a programme emphasises ethics or incentives (or a combination of the two) in its efforts to motivate local participation.' Whereas PFM is often 'sold' as a way of empowering indigenous peoples and local communities by its advocates, in contrast, according to the critics, it injects Western modes of governmentality, disciplinarity and neo-liberalism, implying the *opposite* of empowerment.

7 A Two-World Universe of Forest Governance

This concluding section takes stock of the epistemological, theoretical and empirical analyses and findings of this Element. It addresses philosophical pragmatism and discursive institutionalism, governance discourses and their institutionalisation, forest governance cases and their performances and the Hydra and Chloris worldviews, in order to draw some overall conclusions. The section does so by positing that Hydra – the neo-liberal political economy of deforestation, forest degradation and marginalisation – and Chloris – new modes of governance that partially succeed in changing forest-related practices – are to be considered parallel, but related realities. So, we *refuse* to choose either for a (too) pessimistic, critical account of forest governance, or for an (too) optimistic, mainstream alternative. This synthesis is inspired by the work of International Relations (IR) scholar James Rosenau, particularly his 'bifurcation thesis' (Rosenau, 1988). He depicts world politics as a 'two-world universe': simultaneously state-centric and multicentric. 'Simultaneously' is crucial here, as we need to consider this two-world universe a *duality*, and *not* a dualism. In a similar way, we sketch a two-world universe of forest governance: simultaneously Hydra and Chloris.

7.1 Philosophical Pragmatism and Discursive Institutionalism

This Element builds upon the epistemology of philosophical pragmatism, which advocates theoretical pluralism, mixed methods and critical reflection (see

Section 3). These three characteristics were followed through in this Element by: (1) adopting the perspective of discursive institutionalism (DI), which combines insights from discourse and institutional theories; (2) analysing qualitative and quantitative data of forest governance initiatives, from my own and colleagues' case studies and from systematic literature reviews (SLRs); and (3) confronting the DI perspective with critical theories, such as political economy, neo-liberalisation and governmentality. Whereas the DI perspective tends towards a positively-biased analysis of forest governance (labelled as the Chloris worldview in this Element) the theoretical counterpoints generally do the opposite (here labelled as the Hydra worldview). After all, DI encourages scholars to discover institutionalisation processes of new forest governance ideas, whereas its theoretical counterpoints push scholars to identify political economies, power structures and established interests that maintain the status quo against any serious forest governance reform.

7.2 Governance Discourses and their Institutionalisation

Next, this Element distinguishes three forest governance literatures: (1) governance *modes*, (2) governance *shifts* and (3) governance *norms* (see Section 3). Modes refer to various arrangements among public and private actors to co-govern societal problems and opportunities; shifts include relocations of regulatory authority from public to private actors; and norms refer to criteria and guidelines for good governance (see Sections 4, 5 and 6, respectively). These literatures have emerged from scholarly work – although not out of the blue, because they are based upon empirical observations. Subsequently, the various empirical sections also distinguish more specific governance discourses, such as 'early-modern' and 'late-modern governance', 'governance without government' and 'experimentalist governance', and 'bad', 'good' and 'good enough governance'. Through five case studies, the institutionalisation of these discourses is explored in practice ('the discursive-institutional spiral'; see Section 3).

7.3 Forest Governance Cases and their Performances

The following cases are analysed in this Element: Forest Sector Governance (FSG), Forest Law Enforcement, Governance and Trade (FLEGT), Forest Certification (FC), Reducing Emissions from Deforestation and Forest Degradation (REDD+) and Participatory Forest Management (PFM). Some special attention is given, in line with philosophical pragmatism and DI, to *performance*: did the various governance arrangements indeed work, produce 'real' impacts and contribute to attaining the UN's Global Forest Goals (GFGs)?

In Table 4, I summarise the environmental and social-economic performances of four case studies (the data are derived from the previous sections).[20] The figures in the table show a *potential reach* of those governance initiatives of about 1.4 billion ha of forests in total, which amounts to about 35 per cent of all forests worldwide.[21] This is impressive, but the evidence on the *impact* of these initiatives is either unknown or limited (FLEGT, REDD+), or where aggregated impact data are available, they come with uncertainties and a lack of generalisability (FC, PFM). At this point, what we can conclude is that, to the best of our current knowledge, about half of the impact assessments on FC and PFM report mostly positive impacts for forests and people (and even more so for forests under PFM), whereas the other half report neutral or negative impacts. Hence, the glass is half full and half empty, and here the worldviews come to the fore again. Given the beliefs and theories that one adheres to, what story should take precedence, the fullness of the glass – Chloris, or its emptiness – Hydra?

7.4 Hydra or Chloris?

Hydra is the multi-headed, serpent-like beast that Heracles has to fight to complete his twelve labours in Greek mythology. Every time he chops off a head, it immediately regrows double, and continues attacking him. In this Element, the Hydra metaphor refers to the difficulty of reforming or transforming old state forestry bureaucracies towards new and effective forest governance arrangements, given vested political-economic interests. In contrast, the metaphor of Chloris – the goddess of flowers – is used to sketch an opposite, more optimistic picture of forest governance. 'Let a thousand flowers grow', several of which will definitely bloom. Hence, the message is that forest governance initiatives might indeed make a difference on the ground.

In Section 1, Chloris and Hydra are explored more deeply as multi-layered worldviews on forest governance, including certain beliefs (optimism versus pessimism), theories (problem-solving versus critical) and confirmation biases (data showing that forest governance works or fails). By embracing discursive institutionalism, this Element is without a doubt biased towards the Chloris worldview. As said, DI – being a mainstream theory by its very nature – allows for the possibility of institutional change in politics, policy and governance, in this case through new ideas and discourses. Such a view expresses at least some degree

---

[20] The Netherlands as an example of FSG is excluded from this table because the Dutch forest data are very marginal compared to the four other cases, which are global programmes or initiatives with global exposure.

[21] Compared to 4.059 billion ha of forests worldwide (FAO, 2020). In gross terms, the governance initiatives in Table 4 amount to about 1.5 billion ha, but there is some overlap in forest area among the case studies (see footnote 29).

Table 4 Cases and their performances

Cases	UN Global Forest Goals (GFGs)[22] addressed	Forest area covered (million ha)	Environmental performance[23]	Social-economic performance
FLEGT	1, 5, 6	About 420[24] (15 tropical countries; potential reach)	No data available (as far as is known)	No data available (as far as is known)
FC	1, 2	About 460 (worldwide, but mainly Global North; actual reach)	About half of the assessments identified report positive impact (strong evidence; not to be generalised)[25]	About half of the assessments identified report positive impact (weaker evidence; not to be generalised)[26]

22 See last two paragraphs of Section 1.

23 Performance is equated with impacts or effectiveness in this book. Of course, it would have been interesting to include *cost*-effectiveness as well, whether there is an (im)balance in costs and benefits. But the costs of the various forest governance programmes are very difficult to uncover. Datasets are fragmented (e.g. REDD+) or even absent (e.g. PFM).

24 I use the term 'about' to make readers aware of uncertainty margins. Ideally, I would have calculated such a margin for each figure, but this was not possible given available literature and data sets.

25 Based on Di Girolami (2019). Evidence is considered 'strong' because the general trend in all assessments is confirmed by the subset of most rigorous ones; and evidence is mostly confirmed by the *Mongabay* SLR (see Subsection 5.2). Yet, the overall degree of impact is unknown (can be low, can be high). Moreover, results may not be generalised to the entire world. Finally, I cannot be sure that all impact studies 'out there' were included in the two reviews.

26 Based on the *Mongabay* SLR. Most studies in this part of the review are of a 'less rigorous nature', like observational studies, before–after measurements, surveys and case studies (so no quasi-experiments). Moreover, a comparison with another SLR is lacking. This does not mean, by the way, that these studies are *thus* of low quality, but causal inferences are more difficult to make. Also, these studies only include FSC.

Table 4 (cont.)

Cases	UN Global Forest Goals (GFGs)[22] addressed	Forest area covered (million ha)	Environmental performance[23]	Social-economic performance
REDD+	1, 2, 3, 4	About 43 (>350 projects in 53 tropical countries; actual reach)	Some positive impact reported by a few (mostly rigorous) studies	No data available (as far as is known)
PFM	1, 2, 6	About 600 (worldwide, but mainly in the Global South; actual reach)	About three-quarters of the assessments identified report positive impact (rather strong evidence; not to be generalised)[27]	About half of the assessments identified report positive impact (weaker evidence; not to be generalised)[28]
Overlap		About 100[29]		

---

27 Evidence is considered 'rather strong' because the general trend in all assessments is confirmed by the subset of most rigorous ones, but this SLR could only be weakly confirmed by another (see Subsection 6.3).

28 See footnote 26.

29 The governance initiatives in Table 4 amount to about 1.5 billion ha., but there is some overlap. While exact figures are lacking, I can nonetheless make some estimations. Eleven of the fifteen FLEGT/VPA countries also have certified forest areas, summing up to about 20 million ha. (data derived from the FSC and PEFC websites). Eight of them also apply PFM programmes, summing up to about 15 million ha. (data derived from FAO, 2015, 2016 and RRI, 2014). Overlap between PFM and forest certification is however limited, although community certification exists, probably about 5 million ha. (oral statement of an FSC employee; Molnar (2004) also projects an area of 5 million ha. of community certification in 2020). For REDD+, I do not have data on overlap, but I assume that this will be 100 per cent, hence 43 million ha., since >350 projects are executed in fifty-three countries. The chance that overlap with either one of the other three forest governance initiatives exists is therefore huge (and I know it happens, for example REDD+ and PFM projects). In total, I am then talking about an overlap of 83 million ha., which I level up to about 100 million ha. (because it is very likely that omissions exist here).

of (implicit) optimism and faith in the problem-solving and adaptive capacities of current governance systems. But at the same time, this bias is put into perspective by showing theoretical counterpoints that assume that such governance reform and problem-solving are hard to realise, given established, hegemonic political and economic interests. In terms of empirics, the Element remains inconclusive, by showing the glass as being half full and half empty. Various impact assessments of forest governance initiatives do demonstrate positive performance on the ground, but as many, or even more, fail, particularly in the social-economic realm. So, how to interpret these contrasting data? And who prevails, Chloris or Hydra? Or is this question of 'who prevails' simply wrong? Can it not be *both*, a world of more than one reality?

Empirically, this *both-ness* is not so difficult to understand. After all, FLEGT, FC, REDD+ or PFM might perform very differently under various field situations, depending on political, socio-economic, cultural and ecological characteristics. What works in country A, region B and village C does not necessarily work in country X, region Y and village Z. Governance reform ideas will hardly ever work everywhere in the world. Therefore, failure or partial failure always needs to be factored in. But how to make sense of such plural forest governance realities in theory?

7.5 Bifurcation in World Politics

One way of theorising the Hydra-Chloris dyad is the 'bifurcation thesis' of James Rosenau (1988).[30] Rosenau was an IR scholar who offered a *third way* out of the theoretical schism of the 1980s and 1990s between neo-realists and regime theorists and global governance scholars, neo-pluralists and transnationalists. The main issue was how to interpret the newest developments in the international political economy at that time, such as a remarkable increase in international organisations, laws, regimes, transnational corporations and NGOs; the detente between the capitalist West and the Eastern communist bloc; the emergence of new technologies, like ICT, that facilitated international contacts and interdependencies; and new modes of warfare, like guerrilla and terrorism. One group of scholars (neo-realists, regime theorists) interpreted these developments as changes *within* the given international state system (Keohane, 1984; Waltz, 1979). States are still the ones who decide the course of international affairs for all, irrespective of new actors, regimes, conflicts and technologies entering the scene of international politics. In contrast, a second group of scholars (global governance, neo-pluralists, transnationalists) interpreted these changes as *undermining* the classical state system (Nye and

---

[30] Bifurcation is the division of a phenomenon into two branches or parts from one source.

Donahue, 2000; Strange, 1996). After all, actors other than states increasingly determine outcomes in international affairs, like transnational corporations affecting national economies, international banks instigating financial crises, terrorist groups challenging powerful states, and transnational social movements pushing for stricter international human rights and environmental policies, etc. According to those scholars of the second group, states are losing grip and control.

However, Rosenau (1988) did not consider this theoretical schism very fruitful. For him, both worlds are real, a so-called *two-world universe*, with a 'state-centric world' in which national state actors are primary, existing in parallel with a 'multi-centric' world of diverse, national and international non-state actors, like NGOs, corporations, citizens' groups and scientific organisations.[31] Both worlds bifurcated from the post–World War II, bipolar world order, determined by the USA and the USSR at that time. Subsequently, centralisation tendencies implied a multilateral system led by states, particularly hegemonic states, while decentralisation tendencies led to the rise of transnational actors and relations. Whereas the first system is based on state sovereignty as a source for authority, the second is based on non-state actors' autonomy, legitimacy and performance. Hence, the two systems constitute different 'spheres of authority' (SOAs), but one is not more or less important than the other, according to Rosenau (a conclusion with which neo-realists would of course disagree).

Both systems nonetheless overlap and interact (Rosenau, 1988). Firstly, through people: educated and skilled professionals predominantly in one world (diplomats, civil servants, NGO representatives, scientists, CEOs, etc.), and informed and empowered citizens predominantly in another (civil society, transnational movements, indigenous people). Yet, they move through both worlds, for example at international conferences of the UN (Arts and Babili, 2013). Secondly, parallel complementary diplomacy has emerged in the two worlds, with both classical state diplomacy and 'parallel informal negotiations' among states and non-state actors being present (Buckley et al., 2018). Thirdly, states and non-states do indeed cooperate in international co-governance arrangements, such as in the FLEGT programme (Section 4).

7.6 Conclusion

In a same way, but now applied to forest governance, the two-world universe of Chloris and Hydra can be conceptualised as being bifurcated from the

---

[31] Rosenau dislikes the concept of non-state actor (NSA). He prefers to speak of 'sovereignty-bound' actors (states) and 'sovereignty-free' actors (other actors than states). However, these concepts have never resonated in the discipline of IR, contrary to NSA. Therefore, the latter concept is still used in this book.

traditional state forestry systems of the 1970s.[32] The world of Chloris exhibits the new, partially successful forest governance initiatives that take the shape of co-governance, self-governance and good (enough) forest governance arrangements, which are institutionalised in multiple practices and localities around the world, while enabling many actors to be involved. The world of Hydra, the opposite, expresses the power of traditional political economies and geopolitics that contribute to the continuation of deforestation, forest degradation and marginalisation of forest-dependent people in many regions of the world. Both worlds nonetheless interact, for example through individuals (foresters, land owners, politicians, diplomats, activists), diplomatic practices (round tables on soya, beef and palm oil, for example) and institutional relations (through interdependencies among states, markets and civil societies).

I am not naive. Illegal logging and forest crime do exist on a substantial scale, and still expand in some areas of the world; many political entities and many companies continue to accumulate profits via partially legal and partially illegal routes, and at the cost of forests and people. And, new forest governance discourses and forest management ideas do often fail in practice. But 'good (enough) practices' have institutionalised as well: community certification that benefits both people and forests; timber value chains that have reduced illegalities; community forestry that helps to avoid further deforestation and increases the income of forest-dependent people; and high-value forests that have been restored and expanded. Currently, about 35 per cent of the world's forests are potentially reached by the new governance initiatives dealt with in this Element (FLEGT, FC, REDD+, PFM) and about half of those interventions that were empirically assessed so far produce more or less positive results for forests and/ or people (although this result cannot be generalised to all forest governance initiatives worldwide). Thus Hydra – the political economy and geopolitics of deforestation, degradation and marginalisation – is currently being complemented with Chloris – the world of good (enough) forest governance. And that's the key message of this Element: *both* worlds exist in the current 'forest governance universe'.

---

[32] It would be more consistent with the rest of the book to talk about 'a two-*worldview* universe'. However, this terminology does not sound attractive, so I stick to Rosenau's concept. Moreover, from a pragmatist perspective, a worldview always includes *a world in the material sense*, which *also* implies that a reference to the material world always includes a *view* on it.

References

Abma, T. & in 't Veld, R, eds. (2001). *Handboek beleidswetenschappen: perspectieven, thema's, praktijkvoorbeelden*. Amsterdam: Boom.

Abbott, W. & Snidal, D. (2009). The governance triangle: regulatory standards institutions and the shadow of the state. In W. Mattli & N. Woods, eds., *The Politics of Global Regulation*. Princeton and Oxford: Princeton University Press.

Agrawal, A. (2001). Common property institutions and sustainable governance of resources. *World Development*, **29**(10), 1649–72.

Agrawal, A. (2005). *Environmentality: Technologies of Government and the Making of Subjects*. Durham, NC and London: Duke University Press.

Agrawal, A., Chhatre, A. & Hardin, R. (2008). Changing governance of the world's forests. *Science*, **320**, 1460–2.

Angelsen, A. (2017). REDD+ as result-based aid: general lessons and bilateral agreements of Norway. *Review of Development Economics*, **21**(2), 237–64.

Archer, M. S. (1996). Social integration and system integration: developing the distinction. *Sociology*, **30**, 679–99.

Arnold, J. E. M. (2001). *Forests and People: 25 Years of Community Forestry*. Rome: FAO.

Arnouts, R., van der Zouwen, M. & Arts, B. (2012). Analysing governance modes and shifts in Dutch nature policy. *Forest Policy and Economics*, **16**, 43–50.

Arnstein, S. (1969). A ladder of citizen participation. *Journal of the American Institute of Planners*, **35**(4), 216–24.

Arts, B. (2002). Green alliances of business and NGOs: new styles of self-regulation or dead-end roads? *Corporate Social Responsibility and Environmental Management*, **9**, 26–36.

Arts, B. (2012). Forests policy analysis and theory use: overview and trends. *Forest Policy and Economics*, **16**, 7–13.

Arts, B. (2014). Assessing forest governance from a 'Triple G' perspective: government, governance, governmentality. *Forest Policy and Economics*, **49**, 17–22.

Arts, B. & Babili, I. (2013). Global forest governance: multiple practices of policy performance. In B. Arts, J. Behagel, J. de Koning, et al., eds., *Forest and Nature Governance: A Practice-Based Approach*. Dordrecht: Springer, pp. 111–30.

Arts, B. & Buizer, M. (2009). Forests, discourses, institutions: a discursive-institutional analysis of global forest governance. *Forest Policy and Economics*, **11**(5–6), 340–9.

Arts, B. & de Koning, J. (2017). Community forest management: an assessment and explanation of its performance through QCA. *World Development*, **96**, 315–25.

Arts, B. & Wiersum, F. (2010). Illegal or incompatible? Managing the consequences of timber legality standards on local livelihoods. In Bossman Owusu et al., eds., *Timber Legality, Local Livelihoods and Social Safeguards: Implications of FLEGT/VPA in Ghana*. Kumasi: Tropenbos International Ghana, pp. 6–21.

Arts, B., Lagendijk, A. & van Houtum, H., eds. (2009). *The Disoriented State: Shifts in Governmentality, Territoriality and Governance*. Dordrecht: Springer.

Arts, B., Appelstrand, M., Kleinschmit, D., et al. (2010). Discourses, actors and instruments in international forest governance. In J. Raynor, A. Buck & P. Katila, eds., *Embracing Complexity: Meeting the Challenges of International Forest Governance*. IUFRO World Series Vol. 28, pp.57–74. Vienna: IUFRO.

Arts, B., Behagel, J., de Koning, J., et al. (2014). A practice based approach to forest governance. *Forest Policy and Economics*, **49**, 4–11.

Arts, B., Brockhaus, M. & Ingram V. (2019). The performance of REDD+: from global governance to local practices (editorial). *Forests*, **10**(837), 2–9.

Auld, G. (2014). *Constructing Private Governance: The Rise and Evolution of Forest, Coffee, and Fisheries Certification*. New Haven and London: Yale University Press.

Bachrach, P. & Baratz, M. (1962). Two faces of power. *American Political Science Review*, **56**, 947–52.

Baumgartner, F., Green-Pedersen, C. & Jones, B. (2006). Agenda-setting in comparative perspective. *Journal of European Public Policy*, **13**(7), 959–75.

Baynes, J., Herbohn, J., Smith, C., Fisher, R. & Bray, D. (2015). Key factors which influence the success of community forestry in developing countries. *Global Environmental Change*, **35**, 226–38.

Beck, U., Giddens, A. & Lash, S. (1994). *Reflexive Modernization Politics Tradition and Aesthetics in the Modern Social Order*. Cambridge: Polity.

Beeko, C. & Arts, B. (2010). The EU-Ghana Voluntary Partnership Agreement (VPA): a comprehensive policy analysis. *The International Forestry Review*, **12**(3), 221–30.

Bemelmans-Videc, M., Rist, R. & Vedung, E. (2010). *Carrots, Sticks and Sermons: Policy Instruments and their Evaluation*, 5th ed. Piscataway, NJ: Transaction Publishers.

Bendel, J., ed. (2000). *Terms of Endearment: Business, NGOs and Sustainable Development*. Sheffield: Greenleaf.

Bernstein, R. (2010). *The Pragmatic Turn*. Cambridge: Polity Press.

Bevir, M. (2012). *Governance: A Very Short Introduction*. Oxford: Oxford University Press.

Biermann, F. (2007). 'Earth system governance' as a cross-cutting theme of global change research. *Global Environmental Change*, **17**, 326–37.

Biermann, F. & Gupta, A. (2011). Accountability and legitimacy in earth system governance: a research framework. *Ecological Economics*, **70**, 1856–64.

Biermann, F. & Pattberg, P. (2012). *Global Environmental Governance Reconsidered*. Cambridge, MA: MIT Press.

Birkland, T. (2005). *An Introduction to the Policy Process: Theories, Concepts and Models of Public Policy Making*, 2nd ed. New York and London: M. E. Sharpe.

Blomley T., Kerstin, P., Isango, J., et al. (2008). Seeing the wood for the trees: an assessment of the impact of participatory forest management on forest condition in Tanzania. *Oryx*, **42**(3), 380–391.

Blyth, M. (2002). Institutions and ideas. In Marsh, D. & Stoker, G., eds., *Theory and Methods in Political Science*. New York: Palgrave Macmillan.

Bohman J. (1999). Theories, practices, and pluralism: a pragmatic interpretation of critical social science. *Philosophy of the Social Sciences*, **29**(4), 459–480.

Bose, P., Arts, B. & van Dijk, H. (2012). 'Forest governmentality': a genealogy of subject-making of forest-dependent 'scheduled tribes' in India. *Land Use Policy*, **29**, 664–73.

Bosetti, V. & Lubowski, R. (2010). *Deforestation and Climate Change: Reducing Carbon Emissions from Deforestation and Forest Degradation*. Cheltenham: Edward Elgar.

Bowler, D., Buyung-Ali, L., Healey, J., et al. (2012). Does community forest management provide global environmental benefits and improve local welfare? *Frontiers in Ecology and Environment*, **10**(1), 29–36.

Buckley, K., El-Lakany, H. & Arts, B. (2018). Analyzing the negotiation dynamics leading to the prominence of forests in the Paris Agreement of the UNFCCC. *Journal of Arbitration & Mediation*, **7**(1), 95–127.

Buijs, A., Mattijssen, T. & Arts, B. (2014). The man, the administration and the counter-discourse: an analysis of the sudden turn in Dutch nature conservation policy. *Land Use Policy*, **38**, 676–84.

Butler, R. (2019). Amazon deforestation rises to 11 year high in Brazil (https://news .mongabay.com/2019/11/amazon-deforestation-rises-to-11-year-high-in-brazil/).

Capps, J. (2019). The pragmatic theory of truth. *The Stanford Encyclopedia of Philosophy*, Summer ed., https://plato.stanford.edu/archives/sum2019/ entries/truth-pragmatic/.

Cashore, B. (2002). Legitimacy and the privatization of environmental governance: how non-state market-driven (NSMD) governance systems gain rule-making authority. *Governance* **15**(4), 503–29.

Cashore, B. & Howlett, M. (2007). Punctuating which equilibrium? Understanding thermostatic policy dynamics in Pacific Northwest forestry. *American Journal of Political Science*, **51**(3), 532–51.

Cashore, B. & Stone, M. (2012). Can legality verification rescue global forest governance? Analyzing the potential of public and private policy intersection to ameliorate forest challenges in Southeast Asia. *Forest Policy and Economics*, **18**(2), 13–22.

Cashore, B., Auld, G. & Newson, D. (2004). *Governance through Markets: Forest Certification and the Emergence of Non-State Authority*. New Haven & London: Yale University Press.

Castells, M. (2000). *The Information Age: Economy, Society and Culture*. Volume I, *The Rise of the Network Society*, 2nd ed. Hoboken, NJ: Wiley-Blackwell.

Castree, N. (2010). Neoliberalism and the biophysical environment: a synthesis and evaluation of the research. *Environment & Society* **1**(1), 5–45.

Charnley, S. & Poe, M. (2007). Community forestry in theory and practice: where are we now? *Annual Review of Anthropology*, **36**, 301–36.

Chazdon, R., Brancalion, P., Laestadius, L., et al. (2016). When is a forest a forest? Forest concepts and definitions in the era of forest and landscape restoration. *Ambio*, **45**, 538–50.

Cochran, M. (2002). Deweyan pragmatism and post-positivist social science in IR. *Millennium: Journal of International Studies*, **31**(3), 525–48.

Costanza, R., d'Arge, R., de Groot, R., et al. (1997). The value of the world's ecosystem services and natural capital. *Nature*, **387**, 253–60.

Cooke, B. & Kothari, U., eds. (2001). *Participation: The New Tyranny?* London: Zed Books.

Cox, R. (1981). Social forces, states and world orders: beyond international relations theory. *Millennium: Journal of International Studies*, **10**(2), 126–55.

Crotty, M. (1998). *The Foundations of Social Research: Meaning and Perspective in the Research Process*. London: Sage.

Dean, M. (2010). *Governmentality: Power and Rule in Modern Society*. London: Sage.

Den Besten, J., Arts, B. & Verkooien, P. (2014). The evolution of REDD+: an analysis of discursive-institutional dynamics. *Environmental Science & Policy*, **35**(1), 40–8.

Den Ouden, J. & Muys, B., eds. (2010). *Bosecologie en bosbeheer in de lage landen*. The Hague: Acco Uitgeverij.

Derous, M. & Verhaeghe, E. (2019). When P stands for politics: the role of the EU in the VPAs: a research agenda. *Forest Policy and Economics*, **101**, 81–7.

Di Girolami, E. (2019). Environmental impact of sustainable forest management: two systematic literature reviews of scientific research on the environmental impacts of forest certifications and community forest management at global scale. MSc Thesis, Wageningen: Wageningen University & Research.

Dimitrov, R. (2005). Hostage to norms: states, institutions and global forest politics. *Global Environmental Politics*, **5**(4), 1–24.

Dimitrov, R., Sprinz, D., DiGuisto, G. & Kelle, A. (2007). International non-regimes: a research agenda. *International Studies Review*, **9**, 230–58.

Downs, A. (1972). Up and down with ecology: the issue-attention cycle. *Public Interest*, **28**, 38–50.

Dressler, W., Büscher, B., Schoon, et al. (2010). From hope to crisis and back again? A critical history of the global CBNRM narrative. *Environmental Conservation*, **37**(01), 5–15.

Dryzek, J. (2005). *The Politics of the Earth: Environmental Discourse*s, 2nd ed. Oxford: Oxford University Press.

Dunleavy, P. & Hood, C. (1994). From old public administration to new public management. *Public Money & Management*, **14**(3), 9–16.

Dunn, W. (2016). *Public Policy Analysis: An Introduction*, 5th ed. Hoboken, NJ: Pearson Prentice Hall.

Dupuits, E. & Ongolo, S. (2020). What does autonomy mean for forest communities? The politics of transnational community forestry networks in Mesoamerica and Congo Basin. *World Development Perspectives*, **17**, 100–69.

ECOSOC (2017). *United Nations strategic plan for forests 2017-2030 and quadrennial programme of work of the United Nations Forum on Forests for the period 2017–2020*. Resolution adopted by the Economic and Social Council on 20 April 2017, New York.

FAO (1978). *Forestry for Local Community Development*. Rome: FAO.

FAO (2000). *Global Forest Resources Assessment 2000*. Rome: FAO.

FAO (2005). *Global Forest Resources Assessment 2005*. Rome: FAO.

FAO (2015). *Global Forest Resources Assessment 2015*. Rome: FAO.

FAO (2016). *Forty Years of Community-Based Forestry: A Review of its Extent and Effectiveness*. Rome: FAO.

FAO (2018a). *1948–2018. Seventy Years of FAO's Global Forest Resources Assessment: Historical Overview and Future Prospect*. Rome: FAO.

FAO (2018b). *The State of the World's Forests 2018*. Rome: FAO.

FAO (2020). *Global Forest Resources Assessment 2020*. Rome: FAO.

FAO-PROFOR (2011). *Framework for Assessing and Monitoring Forest Governance*. Rome: FAO; Washington DC: World Bank.

Farber, S., Costanza, R. & Wilson, M. (2002). Economic and ecological concepts for valuing ecosystem services. *Ecological Economics*, **41**, 375–92.

Fernández-Blanco, C., Burns, S. & Giessen, L. (2019). Mapping the fragmentation of the international forest regime complex: institutional elements, conflicts and synergies. *International Environmental Agreements*, **19**, 187–205.

Fischer, F. (2003). *Reframing Public Policy: Discursive Politics and Deliberative Practices*. Oxford: Oxford University Press.

Fletcher, R. (2010). Neoliberal environmentality: towards a poststructuralist political ecology of the conservation debate. *Conservation & Society*, **8**(3), 171–81.

Fletcher, R., Dressler, W., Büscher, B., et al. (2016). Questioning REDD+ and the future of market-based conservation. *Conservation Biology*, **30**, 673–5.

Foucault, M. (1971). *Orders of Discourse*, inaugural address. Paris: College of France.

Foucault, M. (2002). *Power: Essential Work of Foucault 1954–1984*. J. Faubion ed. London: Penguin Books.

Frouws, J. (1994). Mest en macht: een politiek-sociologische studie naar belangenbehartiging en beleidsvorming inzake de mestproblematiek in Nederland vanaf 1970, PhD Diss. Wageningen: Wageningen University.

Fukuyama, F. (1989). The end of history? *The National Interest*, **16**, 3–18.

Geist, H. & Lambin, E. (2002). Proximate causes and underlying driving forces of tropical deforestation. *BioScience*, **52**(2), 143–50.

Giessen, L. (2013). Reviewing the main characteristics of the international forest regime complex and partial explanations for its fragmentation. *International Forestry Review*, **15**(1), 60–70.

Giessen, L. & Buttoud, G. (2014). Special Issue. Assessing forest governance: analytical concepts and their application. *Forest Policy and* Economics, **49**, 1–7.

Gisselquist, R. (2012). What does good governance mean? United Nations University, www.wider.unu.edu/publication/what-does-good-governance-mean.

Goncalves, M., Panjer, M., Greenberg, T., et al. (2012). *Justice for Forests: Improving Criminal Justice Efforts to Combat Illegal Logging*. Washington, DC: World Bank.

Gordon, P. (2017). A vision of Trump at war: how the President could stumble into conflict. *Foreign Affairs*, **96**(3), 10–19.

Grainger, A. (2009). *Controlling Tropical Deforestation*. London: Earthscan.

Grindle, M. (2007). Good enough governance revisited. *Development Policy Review*, **25**(5), 553–74.

Greenpeace International (2021). *Destruction: Certified. Certification; Not a Solution to Deforestation, Forest Degradation and Other Ecosystem Conversion*. Amsterdam: Greenpeace International.

Grober, U. (2012). *Sustainability: A Cultural History*. Totnes: Green Books.

Gupta, A. & Van Asselt, H. (2017). Transparency in multilateral climate politics: furthering (or distracting from) accountability? *Regulation & Governance*, **13**(1), 18–34.

Habermas, J. (1996). *Between Facts and Norms: Contributions to a Discourse Theory of Law and Democracy*. Cambridge: Polity Press.

Hajer, M. (1995). *The Politics of Environmental Discourse: Ecological Modernization and the Policy Process*. Oxford: Oxford University Press.

Hajer, M. & Wagenaar, H. (2003). *Deliberative Policy Analysis: Understanding Governance in the Network Society*. Cambridge: Cambridge University Press.

Hall, P. & Taylor, R. (1996). Political science and the three new institutionalisms. *Political Studies*, **XLIV**, 936–57.

Hansen, C. (2010). Governance of timber resources in the high forest zone of Ghana: a positive political economy perspective, PhD Diss. Copenhagen: University of Copenhagen.

Hansen, M., Stehman, S. & Potapov, P. (2010). Quantification of global gross forest cover loss. *PNAS*, **107**(19), 8650–5.

Hansen, C. & Treue, T. (2008). Assessing illegal logging in Ghana. *International Forestry Review*, **10**(4), 573–90.

Hansen, C., Rutt, R. & Acheampong, E. (2018). 'Experimental' or business as usual? Implementing the European Union Forest Law Enforcement, Governance and Trade (FLEGT) Voluntary Partnership Agreement in Ghana. *Forest Policy and Economics*, **96**, 75–82.

Hardin, G. (1968). The tragedy of the commons. *Science*, **162**(3859), 1243–8.

Hay, C. (2002). *Political Analysis: A Critical Introduction*. Houndmills: Palgrave Macmillan.

Hay, C. (2006). Constructivist institutionalism … or why ideas into interests don't go. Paper presented at the American Political Science Association.

Hay, C., Lister, M. & Marsh, D. (2006). *The State: Theories and Issues*. New York: Palgrave Macmillan.

Held, D. & McGrew, A. (2002). *Governing Globalization: Power, Authority and Global Governance*. Cambridge: Polity Press.

Held, D., Kaldor, M. & Quah, D. (2010). The Hydra-headed crisis. Global Policy Essay (www.globalpolicyjournal.com/articles/global-governance/hydra-headed-crisis).

Heukels, B. (2018). Implementation of FLEGT?VPA in Ghana: legality, traceability and transparency in the timber production chain, MSc Thesis. Wageningen: Wageningen University.

Himes, A. & Muraca, B. (2018). Relational values: the key to pluralistic valuation of ecosystem services. *Current Opinion in Environmental Sustainability*, **35**, 1–7.

Hogl, K., Kvarda, E., Nordbeck, R., et al. (2012). *Environmental Governance: The Challenge of Legitimacy and Effectiveness*. Cheltenham: Edward Elgar.

Hoogeveen, H. & Verkooijen, P. (2010). Transforming sustainable development diplomacy: lessons learned from global forest governance, PhD Diss. Wageningen: Wageningen University.

Hoogerwerf, A. & Herwijerm M. 2008. *Overheidsbeleid: Een inleiding in de beleidswetenschap*, 8th ed. Alphen aan den Rijn: Kluwer.

Howlett, M. (2004). Beyond good and evil in policy implementation: instrument mixes, implementation styles, and second generation theories of policy instrument choice. *Policy and Society*, **23**, 2, 1–17.

Humphreys, D. (1996). *Forest Politics: The Evolution of International Cooperation*. London: Earthscan.

Humphreys, D. (2006). *Logjam: Deforestation and the Crisis of Global Governance*. London: Earthscan.

IDH (The Sustainable Trade Initiative). (2020). *The Urgency of Action to Tackle Tropical Deforestation*. Utrecht: IDH.

Ikenberry, G. (2011). The future of the liberal world order. *Foreign Affairs*, **90**(3), 56–68.

Ilie, A., Apafaian, A., Puiceas, D., et al. (2018). Latest trends in the evolution of PEFC certification. *Scientific Papers Series Management, Economic Engineering in Agriculture and Rural Development*, **18**(3), 179–82.

Jayathilake, H., Prescott, G., Carrasco, L., et al. (2020). Drivers of deforestation and degradation for 28 tropical conservation landscapes. *Ambio*, **112** (1) (online publ: https://doi.org/10.1007/s13280-020-01325-9).

Jeanrenaud, S. (2001). *Communities and Forest Management in Western Europe*. Gland: IUCN.

Jewitt, S. (1995). Europe's 'others'? Forestry policy and practices in colonial and postcolonial India. *Environment and Planning D: Society and Space*, **13**(1), 67–90.

Justus, J., Colyvan, M., Regan, H., et al. (2009). Buying into conservation: intrinsic versus instrumental values. *Trends in Ecology & Evolution*, **24**(4), 187–91.

Kadlec, A. (2006). Reconstructing Dewey: the philosophy of critical pragmatism. *Polity*, **38**(4), 519–42.

Kalamandeen, M., Gloor, E., Mitchard, E., et al. (2018). Pervasive rise of small-scale deforestation in Amazonia. *Nature Scientific Report*, **8**(1600), 1–10.

Keohane, R. (1984). *After Hegemony: Cooperation and Discord in the World Political Economy*. Princeton: Princeton University Press.

Keulartz, J., Schermer, M., Korthals, M., et al. (2004). Ethics in technological culture: a programmatic proposal for a pragmatist approach. *Science, Technology, & Human Values*, **29**(1), 3–29.

Kickert, W., Klijn, E. & Koppejan, J., eds. (1997). *Managing Complex Networks: Strategies for the Public Sector*. London: Sage.

Kingdon, J. (2014). *Agendas, Alternatives, and Public Policies*. Harlow: Pearson.

Kjaer, A. (2004). *Governance*. Cambridge: Polity Press.

Kleinschmit, D., Mansourian, S., Wildburger, C., et al., eds. (2016). Illegal logging and related timber trade: dimensions, drivers, impacts and responses. *IUFRO World Series*, Vol. **35**.

Knill, C. & Liefferink, D. (2013). *Environmental Politics in the European Union: Policy-Making, Implementation and Patterns of Multi-Level Governance*. Manchester: Manchester University Press.

Kolk, A. (1996). *Forests in International Environmental Politics: International Organizations, NGOs and the Brazilian Amazon*. Utrecht: International Books.

Kolk, A. (2000). *Economics of Environmental Management*. Edinburgh: Pearson Education.

Kooiman, J. (2003). *Governing as Governance*. London: Sage.

Krott, M. (2005). *Forest Policy Analysis*. Dordrecht: Springer.

Lemos, M. & Agrawal, A. (2006). Environmental governance. *Annual Review of Environmental Resources*, **31**, 297–325.

Legg, C. (2008). *Pragmatism*. Stanford Encyclopedia of Philosophy (https://plato.stanford.edu/entries/pragmatism/).

Leipold, S. & Winkler, G. (2017). Discursive agency: (re-)conceptualizing actors and practices in the analysis of discursive policymaking. *Policy Studies Journal*, **45**(3), 510–43.

Leipold, S., Sotirov, M., Frei, T., et al. (2016). Protecting 'first world' markets and 'third world' nature: the politics of illegal logging in Australia, the European Union and the United States. *Forest Policy and Economics*, **39**, 294–304.

Lenschow, A., Liefferink, D. & Veenman, S. (2005). When the birds sing: a framework for analysing domestic factors behind policy convergence. *Journal of European Public Policy*, **12**(5), 797–816.

Levin, K., McDermott, C. & Cashore, B. (2008). The climate regime as global forest governance: can Reduced Emissions from Deforestation and Forest Degradation (REDD) initiatives pass a 'dual effectiveness' test? *International Forestry Review*, **10**(3), 538–49.

LNV (Ministerie van Landbouw, Natuur en Voedselkwaliteit). 2020. *Ambities en doelen van Rijk en provincies voor de Bossenstrategie*. The Hague: LNV.

Lyotard, J. (1984). *The Postmodern Condition: A Report on Knowledge*. Minneapolis: University of Minnesota Press.

Maguire, R. (2013). *Global Forest Governance: Legal Concepts and Policy Trends*. Cheltenham: Edward Elgar.

Mann, C. (2018). *The Wizard and the Prophet: Two Remarkable Scientists and their Dueling Visions to Shape Tomorrow's World*. New York: Alfred A. Knopf.

March, J. & Olson, J. (1989). *Rediscovering Institutions*. New York: The Free Press.

Marsh, D. & Stoker, G. (2002). *Theory and Methods in Political Science*. Houndsmill and New York: Palgrave Macmillan.

Marshall, M. & Cole, B. (2011). *Global Report 2011: Conflict, Governance, and State Fragility*. Vienna: Centre for Systemic Peace.

Martone, F. (2010). The emergence of the REDD Hydra: an analysis of the REDD-related discussions and developments in the June session of the UNFCCC and beyond (http://redd-monitor.org/wp-content/uploads/2010/07/redd_hydra_unfccc_jul10_eng.pdf).

Maxcy, S. (2003). Pragmatic threats in mixed method research in the social sciences: the search for multiple modes of inquiry and the end of the philosophy of formalism. In Tashakori, A. & Teddle, V., eds., *Handbook of Mixed Methods in Behavorial and Social Sciences*. London: Sage, pp. 51–89.

Mayers, J. and Bass, S. (2004). *Policy That Works for Forest and People: Real Prospects for Governance and Livelihoods*. London: Earthscan.

McAfee, K. (1999). Selling nature to save it? Biodiversity and green developmentalism. *Environment & Planning D*, **17**(2), 133–54.

McDermott, C., Cashore, B. & Kanowski, P. (2010). *Global Environmental Forest Policies: An International Comparison*. London: Earthscan.

Midtgarden, T. (2012). Critical pragmatism: Dewey's social philosophy revisited. *European Journal of Social Theory*, **15**(4), 505–21.

Miller, E. & Yetiv, S. (2001). The new world order in theory and practice: the Bush administration's worldview in transition. *Presidential Studies Quarterly*, **31**(1), 56–68.

Mol, A., Lauber, V. & Liefferink, D. (2000). *The Voluntary Approach to Environmental Policy: Joint Environmental Approach to Environmental Policy-Making in Europe*. Oxford: Oxford University Press.

Molnar, A. (2004). Forest certification and communities. *International Forestry Review*, **6**(2), 173–80.

Morhen, F. & Vodde, F. (2006). Forests and forestry in the Netherlands. Paper of the Forest Ecology and Management Group. Wageningen: Wageningen University.

Nathan, I., Hansen, C. & Cashore, B. (2014). Timber legality verification in practice: prospects for support and institutionalization. *Forest Policy and Economics*, **48**, 1–5.

Newell, P. (2008). The political economy of global environmental governance. *Review of International Studies*, **34**, 507–29.

Nickerson, R. (1998). Confirmation bias: a ubiquitous phenomenon in many guises. *Review of General Psychology*, **2**(2), 175–220.

North, D. (1990). *Institutions, Institutional Change and Economic Performance.* Cambridge: Cambridge University Press.

Nye, J. & Donahue, J., eds. (2000). *Governance in a Globalizing World.* Washington, DC: Brookings.

Osborne, D. & Gaebler, T. (1992). *Reinventing Government: How the Entrepreneurial Spirit is Transforming the Public Sector.* New York: Plume.

Ostrom, E. (1990). *Governing the Commons: The Evolution of Institutions for Collective Action.* Cambridge: Cambridge University Press.

Overdevest, C. & Zeitlin J. (2014). Assembling an experimentalist regime: transnational governance interactions in the forest sector. *Regulation & Governance*, **8**, 22–48.

Park, J., Conca, K. & Finger, M. (2008). *The Crisis of Global Environmental Governance: Towards a New Political Economy of Sustainability.* London: Routledge.

Pattberg, P. (2007). *Private Institutions and Global Governance: The New Politics of Environmental Sustainability.* Cheltenham: Edward Elgar.

Pearce, F. (2018). Conflicting data: how fast is the world losing its forests? *Yale Environment* **360** (https://e360.yale.edu/features/).

Phelps, J., Webb, E. & Agrawal, A. (2010). Does REDD+ threaten to recentralize forest governance? *Science*, **328**, 312–13.

Peters, G., Piere, J. & King, D. (2005). The politics of path dependency: political conflict in historical institutionalism. *The Journal of Politics*, **67**, 1275–300.

Phillips, N., Lawrence, T. B. & Hardy, C. (2004). Discourse and institutions. *Academy of Management Review*, **29**, 635–52.

Pierre, J., ed. (2000). *Debating Governance: Authority, Steering and Democracy.* Oxford: Oxford University Press.

Pierre, J. & Peters, G. (2000). *Governance, Politics and the State*. London: Macmillan.

Proctor, J. (1998). The social construction of nature: relativist accusations, pragmatist and critical realist responses. *Annals of the Association of American Geographers*, **88**(3), 352–76.

Pülzl, H., Hogl, K., Kleinschmit, D., et al. (2013). *European Forest Governance: Issues at Stake and the Way Forward*. Bonn: European Forest Institute.

Rabe, B. (2007). Beyond Kyoto: climate change policy in multilevel governance systems. *Governance*, **20**(3), 423–44.

Rayner, J., Buck, A. & Katila, P., eds. (2010). Embracing complexity: meeting the challenges of international forest governance. *IUFRO World Series*, Vol **28**.

Rhodes, R. (1996). The new governance: governing without government. *Political Studies*, **XLIV**, 652–67.

Rittberger, V., ed. (1993). *Regime Theory and International Relations*. Oxford: Clarendon Press.

Rosenau, J. (1988). Patterned chaos in global life: structure and process in the two worlds of world politics. *International Political Science Review*, **9**(4), 327–64.

Rosenau, J. & Czempiel, E., eds. (1992). *Governance without Government: Order and Change in World Politics*. Cambridge: Cambridge University Press.

RRI (Rights & Resources Initiative). (2014). *What Future for Reform? Progress and Slowdown of Forest Tenure Reform since 2002*. Washington, DC: RRI.

Rutt, R., Myers, R., Ramcilovic-Suominen, S., et al. (2018). FLEGT: another 'forestry fad'? *Environmental Science & Policy*, **89**, 266–72.

Sabatier, P. ed. (2007). *Theories of the Policy Process*, 2nd ed. Oxford: Westview Press.

Sabel, C. & Zeitlin, J. (2012). Experimentalist governance. In D. Levi-Four, ed., *The Oxford Handbook on Governance*. Oxford: Oxford University Press, pp. 169–85.

Savenije, H. & van Dijk, K. (2010). *World Forestry at a Crossroad: Going Alone or Joining with Others*. Wageningen: Tropenbos International.

Schanz, H. (2002). National forest programmes as discursive institutions. *Forest Policy and Economics*, **4**(4), 269–79.

Schmidt, V. (2002). Does discourse matter in the politics of welfare state adjustment? *Comparative Political Studies*, **35**(2), 168–93.

Schmidt, V. (2005). Institutionalism and the state. In C. Hay, D. Marsh & M. Lister, eds., *The State: Theories and Issues*. Basingstoke, Palgrave, pp. 98–117.

Schmidt, V. (2008). Discursive institutionalism: the explanatory power of ideas and discourse. *Annual Review of Political Science*, **11**, 303–26.

Scott, J. (1998). *Seeing like a State: How Certain Schemes to Improve the Human Condition Have Failed*. Cambridge, MA: Yale University Press.

Sergent, A., Arts, B. & Edwards, P. (2018). Governance arrangements in the European forest sector: shifts towards 'new governance' or maintenance of state authority? *Land Use Policy*, **79**, 968–76.

Simonet, G., Bos, A., Duchelle A., et al. (2018). Forests and carbon: the impacts of local REDD+ initiatives. In A. Angelsen, C. Martius C., De Sy, V. et al., eds., *Transforming REDD+: Lessons and New Directions*. Bogor: CIFOR, pp. 117–30.

Somorin, A. (2014). Governing Congo Basin forests in a changing climate: actors, discourses and institutions for adaptation and mitigation, PhD Diss. Wageningen: Wageningen University.

Sotirov, M., Pokorny, B., Kleinschmit, D., et al. (2020). International forest governance and policy: institutional architecture and pathways of influence in global sustainability. *Sustainability*, **12**, 1–25.

Soto Golcher, C. (2020). Lazy lands or carbon sinks? Frames and integration in the nexus of forest, agriculture and climate change. PhD Diss. Wageningen: Wageningen University.

Springate-Baginski, O. & Wollenberg, E. (2010). *REDD, Forest Governance and Rural Livelihoods: The Emerging Agenda*. Bogor: CIFOR.

Steurer, R. 2013. Disentangling governance: a synoptic view of regulation by government, business and civil society. *Policy Science*, **46**, 387–410.

Strange, S. (1996). *The Retreat of the State: The Diffusion of Power in the World Economy*. Cambridge: Cambridge University Press.

Streeck, W. & Thelen, K. (2005). *Beyond Continuity: Institutional Change in Advanced Political Economies*. Oxford: Oxford University Press.

Tashakkori, A. & Teddlie, C. (1998). Pragmatism and the choice of research strategy. In Tashakkori, A. & Teddlie, C. *SAGE Handbook of Mixed Methods in Social & Behavioral Research*, 1st ed. London: Sage, pp. 21–39.

Tashakkori, A. & Teddlie, C. (2010). *SAGE Handbook of Mixed Methods in Social & Behavioral Research*, 2nd ed. London: Sage.

Teorell, J. (2006). Political participation and three theories of democracy: a research inventory and agenda. *European Journal of Political Research*, **45**(5), 787–810.

Turnhout, E., Gupta, A., Weatherley-Sing, J., et al. (2017). Envisioning REDD+ in a post-Paris era: between evolving expectations and current practice. *WIREs Climate Change*, **8**(1), 1–13.

Umans, L. (1993). A discourse on forestry science. *Agriculture and Human Values*, **Fall**, 26–40.

UNFCCC (2010). *Report of the Conference of the Parties on its Sixteenth Session, Held in Cancun from 29 November to 10 December 2010*. Bonn: UNFCCC Secretariat.

Van de Graaf, H. & Hoppe, R. (1996). *Beleid en Politiek : Een inleiding tot de beleidswetenschappen en beleidskunde*. Bussum: Coutinho.

Van den Brink, M. & Metze, T. (2006). *Words Matter in Policy and Planning: Discourse Theory and Method in the Social Sciences*. Utrecht: Netherlands Graduate School of Urban and Regional Research.

Van der Steen, M., Faber, A., Frankowski, A., et al. (2018). *Opgavegericht evalueren: Beleidsevaluatie voor systeemverandering*. The Hague: NSOB.

Van der Ven, H. & Cashore, B. (2018). Forest certification: the challenge of measuring impacts. *Current Opinion in Environmental Sustainability*, **32**, 104–11.

Van Kersbergen, K & van Waarden, F. (2004). 'Governance' as a bridge between disciplines: cross-disciplinary inspiration regarding shifts in governance and problems of governability, accountability and legitimacy. *European Journal of Political Research*, **43**, 143–71.

Van Tatenhove, J., Arts, B. & Leroy, P., eds. (2000). *Political Modernization and the Environment: The Renewal of Policy Arrangements*. Dordrecht: Kluwer Academic Publishers.

Van Waarden, F. (1992). Dimensions and types of policy networks. *European Journal of Political Research*, **21**(1–2), 29–52.

Vandergeest, P. & Peluso, N. (2006). Empires of forestry: professional forestry and state power in Southeast Asia, Part 1. *Environment and History*, **12**, 31–64.

Veenman, S., Liefferink, D. & Arts B. (2009). A short history of Dutch forest policy: the 'de-institutionalisation' of a policy arrangement. *Forest Policy and Economics*, **11**, 202–8.

Vidal, J. (2020). Tip of the iceberg: is our destruction of nature responsible for Covid-19? *Guardian*, 18 March 2020.

Visseren-Hamakers, I., McDermott, C., Vijge, M., et al. (2012). Trade-offs, co-benefits and safeguards: current debates on the breadth of REDD+. *Current Opinion on Environmental Sustainability*, **4**(6), 646–53.

Visseren-Hamakers, I. & Pattberg, P. (2013). We can't see the forest for the trees. the environmental impact of global forest certification is unknown. *Gaia*, **22**(1), 25–8.

Waltz, K. (1979). *Theory of International Politics*. New York: McGraw-Hill.

Waters, M. (1995). *Globalization*. London: Routledge.

Webb, M. & Krasner, S. (1989). Hegemonic stability theory: an empirical assessment. *Review of International Studies*, **15**, 183–98.

Weiss, T. (2000). Governance, good governance and global governance: conceptual and actual challenges. *Third World Quarterly*, **21**(5), 795–814.

Wiersum, F. (1995). 200 years of sustainability in forestry: lessons from history. *Environmental Management* **19**(3), 321–9.

Wiersum, F. (2009). Community forestry between local autonomy and global encapsulation: *quo vadis* with environmental and climate change payments? Paper presented at the First Community Forestry International Workshop, Pokhara, Nepal, September 15–18.

Wiersum, F., Humphries, S. & van Bommel, S. (2011). Certification of community forestry enterprises: experiences with incorporating community forestry in a global system for forest governance. *Small-Scale Forestry*, **12**(1), 15–31.

Wiersum, F. & Arts, B. (2013). International forest policy. In Sands, R., ed., *Forestry in a Global Context*, 2nd ed. Wallingford, UK and Boston, MA: CABI, 218–32.

Winkler, G., Leipold, S., Buhmann, K., et al. (2017). Narrating illegal logging across the globe: between green protectionism and sustainable resource use. *International Forestry Review*, **19**(S1), 81–97.

Woods, N. (2000). The challenge of good governance for the IMF and the World Bank themselves. *World Development*, **28**(5), 823–41.

Work, R. (2002). Overview of decentralization worldwide: a stepping stone to improved governance and human development. *Philippine Journal of Public Administration*, **XLVI**(1–4), 1–24.

Xiao-Peng, S., Hansen, M., Stehman, S., et al. (2018). Global land change from 1982 to 2016. *Nature*, **560**, 639–43.

Acknowledgements

The author wishes to thank the following persons for their contributions to the structure and contents of the manuscript: Noelle Aarts, Jelle Behagel, Erica Di Girolami, Gina Maffey (language editor), Frits Mohren, Duncan Liefferink, Laurent Umans, the editors and technical assistants of the Elements series, two anonymous reviewers and many colleagues from the forest governance research community (too many to refer to individually). The author is also grateful to the Institute for Science in Society at Radboud University Nijmegen for offering office space and intellectual inspiration to work on this Element one day a week in 2019 and 2020 (until Covid-19 hit the Netherlands).

About the Author

Professor Bas Arts' research and teaching focus on international forest, biodiversity and climate change governance, local natural resource management and their interconnections. He has (co)produced over 150 academic publications, including journal articles, books, book chapters and reports (since 1989). Since 2006, forty PhDs graduated under his (co)supervision.

www.wur.nl/nl/Personen/Bas-prof.dr.-BJM-Bas-Arts.htm

https://scholar.google.nl/citations?user=8Ais1VUAAAAJ&hl=nl&oi=ao

Cambridge Elements ☰

Earth System Governance

Frank Biermann
Utrecht University

Frank Biermann is Research Professor of Global Sustainability Governance with the Copernicus Institute of Sustainable Development, Utrecht University, the Netherlands. He is the founding Chair of the Earth System Governance Project, a global transdisciplinary research network launched in 2009; and Editor-in-Chief of the new peer-reviewed journal *Earth System Governance* (Elsevier). In April 2018, he won a European Research Council Advanced Grant for a research program on the steering effects of the Sustainable Development Goals.

Aarti Gupta
Wageningen University

Aarti Gupta is Professor of Global Environmental Governance at Wageningen University, The Netherlands. She is Lead Faculty and a member of the Scientific Steering Committee of the Earth System Governance (ESG) Project and a Coordinating Lead Author of its 2018 Science and Implementation Plan. She is also principal investigator of the Dutch Research Council-funded TRANSGOV project on the Transformative Potential of Transparency in Climate Governance. She holds a PhD from Yale University in environmental studies.

About the Series

Linked with the Earth System Governance Project, this exciting new series will provide concise but authoritative studies of the governance of complex socio-ecological systems, written by world-leading scholars. Highly interdisciplinary in scope, the series will address governance processes and institutions at all levels of decision-making, from local to global, within a planetary perspective that seeks to align current institutions and governance systems with the fundamental 21st Century challenges of global environmental change and earth system transformations.

Elements in this series will present cutting edge scientific research, while also seeking to contribute innovative transformative ideas towards better governance. A key aim of the series is to present policy-relevant research that is of interest to both academics and policy-makers working on earth system governance.
More information about the Earth System Governance project can be found at: www.earthsystemgovernance.org

Cambridge Elements ☰

Earth System Governance

Printed in the United States
by Baker & Taylor Publisher Services